say it with
cake

say it with cake

cake

EDD KIMBER

Celebrate with over 80 cakes,
cookies, pies, and more

KYLE BOOKS

PHOTOGRAPHY BY GEORGIA GLYNN SMITH • DESIGN BY ANITA MANGAN

Published in 2013 by Kyle Books
an imprint of Kyle Cathie Ltd.
www.kylebooks.com
Distributed by National Book Network
4501 Forbes Blvd., Suite 200
Lanham, MD 20706
Phone: (800) 462-6420

First published in Great Britain in 2012 by
Kyle Books
an imprint of Kyle Cathie Ltd.

ISBN: 978-1-906868-93-2

Text © 2012 Edd Kimber
Photographs © 2012 Georgia Glynn Smith
Design © 2012 Kyle Books

Editor: Catharine Robertson
Designer: Anita Mangan
Photographer: Georgia Glynn Smith
Photographer's assistant: Sue Prescott
Food and props stylist: Anna Jones
Food stylist's assistants: Emily Ezekiel, Zoe Allen, and Becky Bax
Copy editor: Jan Cutler
Proofreader: Jane Bamforth
Index: Helen Snaith
Production: Nic Jones and Gemma John

Library of Congress Control No: 2013938133

Printed and bound in China by C&C Offset Printing Company Ltd.

contents

**To Matt,
my wonderful
partner and
best friend**

Think of a special occasion and I bet there'll be a cake or dessert that is associated with it. For Thanksgiving you have Pecan Pie, for birthday parties you have the classic yellow cake with chocolate frosting and so on and so forth. In my mind you can't have a big celebration without either a big slice of cake or something sweet and delicious to dig into—the two just go hand in hand.

I love baking and I love it because you rarely bake for yourself. I can't remember the last time I baked myself a cake and didn't share it with someone else, and it's with this spirit that I have written this book. I hope that throughout the year, whatever the occasion, there is something in these pages that will fit the bill and give everyone a little bit of happiness, as every cake should.

For me, baking is about flavor first and foremost—looks come second—but when you're serving it for a special occasion it's even better when the finished product looks stunning. I am not a natural cake decorator so I have designed all of these recipes to look beautiful whilst still being easy to achieve. If I can do it, so can you!

Many of the recipes in this book are inspired by memories from when I was a kid. I can always remember the cakes we had for birthdays and holidays and they hold a very special place in my heart. I hope that the recipes here will in turn become part of your family repertoire and help you to create your own memories that will last for years to come.

Happy Baking,
Edd x

Useful Equipment

Baking Sheets

I prefer to use heavy-duty light colored pans, which can be bought inexpensively from restaurant supply shops and some kitchenware shops. Dark and flimsy baking sheets tend to bake unevenly and brown the bottom of whatever is baking on them too fast, whereas heavy-duty light colored pans usually bake nice and evenly. I also prefer baking sheets that have a lip around the edge for their versatility.

Cake/Loaf Pans

In general I prefer to use light colored bakeware; it is normally better quality and bakes cakes more evenly. For the recipes in this book you will need a variety of pans—the specific sizes are listed in each recipe. A good place to start is with a set of three 8in pans, about 2in deep.

Bundt Pans

There a few recipes in this book that use either a bundt or bundlette pan. I prefer those made by Nordicware, but if you don't want to purchase extra pans, all the recipes in this book can be baked in regular pans, you would just need to adjust the timings.

Cake Turntable

While this isn't a necessity, it does make the job of decorating cakes a lot easier. If you do decide to get one there is no need to spend a lot—the cheaper plastic models will work for everything in this book.

Cookie Cutters

Only a few of my recipes use cookie cutters and for that purpose a small set of plain round cutters in multiple sizes is the main thing you will need. There are also two recipes that use specially shaped cutters, shaped to look like wedding cakes and Christmas tree decorations. In general, cookie cutters are very cheap and can often be purchased for just a few dollars.

Electric Stand Mixer

I use my Kitchenaid almost every single day and it really makes baking so much more efficient and easy. If you do a lot of baking, I can't recommend an electric mixer any more highly. If you prefer to make things by hand that is fine of course, but be aware that recipes in this book have been tested using electric mixers, both stand and hand varieties, so may take longer to make.

Food Processor

I love my food processor as it makes certain jobs so much easier. While not strictly required, there are certain recipes that might be difficult to make without one.

Measuring Spoons

When a recipe calls for a teaspoon of baking powder it means a level teaspoon–an accurate measure that you can't get with the teaspoon you use to make your cup of coffee. Invest a couple of dollars and get yourself a set of measuring spoons. Most supermarkets sell them these days.

9

Mixing Bowls

I prefer to use a set of Pyrex bowls for baking because they are cheap, heatproof, and durable, just what you need for baking. I prefer not to use plastic as they tend to retain a film of fat even after being washed, which is especially bad when making meringue.

Offset Spatula

Other than a cake turntable this is the best thing I can suggest to make decorating your cakes easier. Spreading frosting across the tops and sides of cakes is much easier using one of these spatulas as it gives more control and lifts your hand an inch away from the cake making it easier to get a flat surface.

Piping Bags

These are invaluable for piping out macaron batter in perfect little rounds but are also useful for piping choux pastry or royal icing. I prefer to use the disposable type as it makes for much easier clean up.

Rolling Pin

This is a necessity for rolling out fondant to cover your cakes. I prefer to use a large polythene model as it very smooth, which means smoother fondant when rolling it out.

Sugar Thermometer

Where a recipe indicates that a sugar syrup needs to be cooked to a specific degree, a sugar, or candy, thermometer is needed to achieve this accuracy. I prefer to use a Thermapen, a quick-read digital probe thermometer.

Wire racks

I never seem to have enough wire racks and it's only when you don't have any that you realize how useful these are. A set of three should be all you really need.

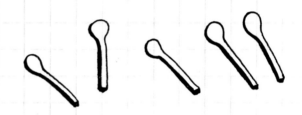

birthdays & parties

Strawberry Shortcake

SERVES 12-15

butter, for greasing
5 **large eggs**
⅔ cup **superfine sugar**
1 tsp **vanilla extract**
1 cup **all-purpose flour**
2 tbsp **unsalted butter**,
   melted and cooled
2½lb **strawberries**,
   hulled and quartered
confectioners' sugar,
   for dusting

For the vanilla syrup
1¼ cups **superfine sugar**
1 tsp **vanilla bean paste**

**For the vanilla
whipped cream**
2 cups **heavy cream**
½ tsp **vanilla bean paste**
2 tsp **confectioners' sugar**

What better cake could you serve during the summer, when strawberries are at their best, than this towering beauty? A light sponge cake is filled with freshly whipped cream, and lots and lots of strawberries—I can't think of anything better. The cake uses a genoise sponge, which is very easy to make, just follow the steps and you will have a wonderfully light cake.

1. Preheat the oven to 350°F, then grease and line two 8in cake pans with parchment paper, greasing the parchment too.

2. Put the eggs, sugar, and vanilla in a heatproof bowl set over a pan of gently simmering water, making sure the bowl doesn't touch the water. Whisk constantly until the sugar has dissolved and the mixture is just warm to the touch. Remove the bowl from the pan and, using an electric mixer, beat for 5 minutes on high speed, then reduce the speed to medium and beat for another 3 minutes. By this stage the mixture should have tripled in volume, and when the beaters are lifted from the bowl they should form a slowly dissolving ribbon.

3. Sift in the flour and gently fold together, making sure all the flour is combined, but trying to keep as much volume as possible. Take a large spoonful of the batter and add it to the melted butter, then mix together (this will lighten the butter and help to incorporate it into the batter). Gently fold this into the batter.

4. Divide the batter equally between the prepared pans and gently level out. Bake for 25 minutes or until risen and golden, or when a skewer inserted into the center of the cake comes out clean. Allow the cakes to cool in the pans for 10 minutes before turning onto a wire rack to cool completely.

5. To make the syrup, put the sugar and 1 cup water in a small pan and bring to a boil, then simmer for a few minutes until the sugar has dissolved. Remove from the heat and stir in the vanilla paste.

6. To make the vanilla whipped cream, put the cream, vanilla, and sugar into a large bowl and whisk until the cream forms soft peaks.

7. To assemble the cake, use a serrated knife to slice each cake into two layers and put the first layer on a cardboard cake board or serving plate. Brush with a generous amount of syrup and top with just under a quarter of the strawberries and a third of the whipped cream. Repeat with the other layers and top the finished cake with the remaining strawberries, a final drizzle of syrup and dust with a little confectioners' sugar for decoration.

TIP

As this cake is filled with whipped cream, it is best served as soon as it is assembled.

Luscious Lemon Cake

SERVES 12

1 cup **unsalted butter**,
  at room temperature,
  plus extra for greasing
2¼ cups **all-purpose flour**
⅓ cup **cornstarch**
4½ tsp **baking powder**
½ tsp **salt**
2 cups **superfine sugar**
2 tsp **vanilla extract**
4 medium **eggs**, separated
1¼ cups **whole milk**

For the lemon Italian meringue buttercream
1¼ cups **superfine sugar**
6 medium **egg whites**
2 cups **unsalted butter**,
  at room temperature
¾ cup **lemon curd**
  (available at gourmet
  supermarkets)
yellow gel food coloring

This would be the perfect birthday cake for my mother. She loves lemon, and this cake is full of that gorgeous zesty lemon flavor. The bright frosting turns the cake into something a little more elegant—and don't worry, it's really easy to achieve.

1. Preheat the oven to 350°F, then grease and line three 8in round cake pans with parchment paper, greasing the parchment too. In a medium bowl, whisk the flour, cornstarch, baking powder, and salt together to combine, then set aside. Put the butter in a large bowl and, using an electric mixer, beat on medium-high speed until smooth and light. Add the sugar and beat until light and fluffy, about 5 minutes.

2. Add the vanilla and mix to combine. With the mixer on medium speed, add the egg yolks, one at a time, beating until fully combined before adding the next. With the mixer on low, sift in the flour mixture in three additions, alternating with the milk, starting and finishing with the flour.

3. Pour the egg whites into a clean, grease-free bowl and whisk until they hold soft peaks. Add the whites to the cake batter and gently fold together until just combined and there are no streaks of white.

4. Divide the batter evenly between the prepared pans and bake for 30–35 minutes or until the cakes are golden brown and spring back when lightly touched. Allow the cakes to cool in the pans for 10 minutes before turning onto a wire rack to cool completely.

5. To make the buttercream, put ½ cup water and the sugar in a pan over medium heat, and have a sugar thermometer ready. Pour the egg whites into a clean, grease-free bowl (this is best done using a freestanding electric mixer). As the syrup reaches about 240°F, start beating the whites on high speed. Cook until the syrup registers 250°F, then remove from the heat and, with the mixer still running, pour the syrup in a slow stream down the side of the bowl containing the whites, avoiding the beaters. Continue beating on high speed until the meringue is at room temperature.

6. With the mixer on medium-high speed, add the butter, a few pieces at a time, beating until fully combined. When adding the butter it can sometimes look curdled; if this happens, don't worry, just keep mixing and eventually it will smooth out again forming a light buttercream. Add half the lemon curd and mix to combine.

7. To assemble the cake, put the first cake layer on a cardboard cake board or serving plate and top with a layer of the buttercream. Spread half the remaining lemon curd on top, leaving a ¾in border around the edge. Top with the second cake layer and repeat as before, then top with the last layer of cake.

8. To finish the cake, take a third of the remaining buttercream and add a little yellow food coloring so that there is a strong contrast between the two batches. Take the yellow buttercream and apply around the bottom third of the cake. This can either be done with a small offset spatula or a piping bag. Take the remaining buttercream and apply to the top and remaining two-thirds of the sides.

9. Using a spoon or spatula, draw a swirl pattern around the sides of the cake, this will slightly blend the two colors creating a beautiful gradient, like a sunset. Repeat the swirl on the top of the cake.

16

White Chocolate Rainbow Cake

SERVES 18

1 cup **unsalted butter**,
  at room temperature,
  plus extra for greasing
2¼ cups **all-purpose flour**
⅓ cup **cornstarch**
4½ tsp **baking powder**
½ tsp **salt**
2 cups **superfine sugar**
2 tsp **vanilla extract**
4 medium **eggs**, separated
1¼ cups **whole milk**

gel food coloring in red,
  yellow, orange, purple,
  blue, and green

**For the white chocolate
Italian meringue frosting**
5½oz **white chocolate**
1½ cups **superfine sugar**
6 medium **egg whites**
2 cups + 6 tbsp **unsalted
  butter**, at room temperature

This cake is a monster—it has six layers and uses a lot of butter, but do keep in mind that it will serve a lot of people, and it will make a spectacular cake for a birthday or any other occasion. The beauty of this cake is that, apart from being rather large, it looks quite innocent from the outside, because the white frosting hides the multicolored rainbow inside. Imagine people's reactions when it is first cut into—it's well worth the effort.

1. Preheat the oven to 350°F, then grease and line three 8in round cake pans with parchment paper, greasing the parchment too. In a medium bowl, whisk the flour, cornstarch, baking powder, and salt together to combine, then set aside.

2. Put the butter in a large bowl and, using an electric mixer, beat on medium-high speed until smooth and light. Add the sugar and beat until light and fluffy, about 5 minutes, then add the vanilla and mix to combine. With the mixer on medium speed, add the egg yolks, one at a time, beating each until fully combined before adding the next. With the mixer on low, sift in the flour mixture in three additions, alternating with the milk, starting and finishing with the flour.

3. Pour the egg whites into a clean, grease-free bowl and whisk until they hold soft peaks. Add the whites to the cake batter and gently fold together until just combined and there are no streaks of white. Divide the batter equally between six small bowls. Add a small amount of each coloring to each bowl, enough to make it a vibrant color. Add the first three bowls to the prepared pans and bake for 15 minutes or until they spring back when lightly touched. Let cool in the pans for 10 minutes before turning onto a wire rack to cool completely. Repeat with the remaining three portions of batter.

4. To make the frosting, melt the chocolate in a heatproof bowl set over a pan of gently simmering water, making sure the bottom of the bowl doesn't touch the water. Remove from the heat and let cool.

5. Put ⅔ cup water and the sugar in a pan over medium heat. Bring to a boil and have a sugar thermometer ready. Meanwhile, pour the egg whites into a clean, grease-free bowl (this is best done using a freestanding electric mixer). Start beating the whites on high speed when the syrup in the pan reaches about 240°F on the sugar thermometer. Cook until the syrup registers 250°F. With the mixer still running, pour the syrup in a slow stream down the side of the bowl containing the whites, avoiding the beaters. Continue beating on high speed until the meringue is at room temperature. With the mixer on medium-high speed, add the butter a few pieces at a time, beating until fully combined. When adding the butter it can sometimes look curdled; if this happens don't worry, just keep mixing and eventually it will smooth out to form a light buttercream frosting. With the mixer on medium speed, pour in the melted chocolate and mix until fully combined.

6. To assemble the cake, put the purple cake layer on a cardboard cake board or serving plate and top with a thin layer of frosting. Repeat the process with the other cake layers in the order of a rainbow (purple, blue, green, yellow, orange, red) and then spread the remaining frosting across the top and sides of the cake.

18

Tiramisu Charlotte

SERVES 15

2 tbsp **unsalted butter**,
  melted and cooled, plus
  extra butter for greasing
4 large **eggs**
½ cup **superfine sugar**
¾ cup **all-purpose flour**

For the mascarpone mixture
4 large **eggs**, separated
¾ cup **superfine sugar**
9oz **mascarpone**

For the coffee syrup
⅔ cup strong **coffee**,
  preferably espresso
4 tbsp **Marsala** or **Madeira**,
  or to taste

To finish
cocoa powder, for dusting
7oz **ladyfingers**
3½oz **dark chocolate**
  (about 70% cocoa solids),
  in one piece

I absolutely love tiramisu—it's a dish I will almost always order in a good Italian restaurant, but it's not always the most attractive dessert in the world. My more elegant take on the traditional recipe is in the form of a charlotte, which makes it even more special and suitable for any occasion. To create an even prettier presentation, wrap the whole cake in a piece of ribbon.

1. Preheat the oven to 350°F, then grease and line an 8in cake pan with parchment paper, greasing the parchment too. Put the eggs and sugar in a heatproof bowl set over a pan of gently simmering water, making sure the bottom of the bowl doesn't touch the water. Whisk constantly until the sugar has dissolved and the mixture is just warm to the touch.

2. Remove the bowl from the pan and, using an electric mixer, beat for 5 minutes on high speed, then reduce the speed to medium and beat for another 3 minutes. By this stage the mixture should have tripled in volume, and when the beaters are lifted from the bowl they should form a slowly dissolving ribbon.

3. Sift in the flour and gently fold together, making sure all the flour is combined, but trying to keep as much volume as possible. Take a large spoonful of the batter and add it to the melted butter, then mix together (this will lighten the butter and help to incorporate it into the batter). Gently fold this into the batter.

4. Pour the batter into the prepared pan and gently level out. Bake for 25 minutes or until the cake is risen and golden, or when a skewer inserted into the middle of the cake comes out clean. Let cool in the pan for 10 minutes before turning onto a wire rack to cool completely.

5. To make the mascarpone mixture, beat the egg yolks and ½ cup of the superfine sugar until pale and creamy, then add the mascarpone and beat until smooth. Pour the egg whites into a clean, grease-free bowl and whisk until they form soft peaks. Slowly add the remaining sugar and whisk to form firm peaks. Gently fold the meringue into the mascarpone mixture and set aside. To make the coffee syrup, mix the coffee and Marsala together in a small bowl.

6. To assemble the cake, use a serrated knife to slice the cake into three layers, then put the first layer into the bottom of a 9in springform cake pan. Brush the top with about a third of the coffee syrup and top with just under half the mascarpone mixture. Dust the mascarpone with about 1 heaping teaspoon cocoa powder. Repeat the process with the second layer of cake.

7. Press the ladyfingers down around the sides of the pan, then add the final layer of cake to the top and gently press down (this will help to stick the ladyfingers to the cake). Brush with the coffee and top with the remaining mascarpone mixture, gently leveling it out. Chill the cake for 4 hours. Just before serving, use a sharp knife or a vegetable peeler to grate the bar of chocolate to create shavings. Top the cake with the chocolate shavings, then remove the springform collar.

Lemon Present Cake

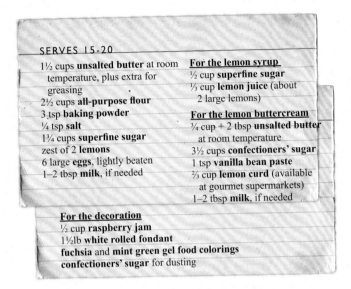

SERVES 15-20

1½ cups **unsalted butter** at room temperature, plus extra for greasing
2½ cups **all-purpose flour**
3 tsp **baking powder**
¼ tsp **salt**
1¾ cups **superfine sugar**
zest of 2 **lemons**
6 large **eggs**, lightly beaten
1–2 tbsp **milk**, if needed

For the lemon syrup
½ cup **superfine sugar**
⅓ cup **lemon juice** (about 2 large lemons)

For the lemon buttercream
¾ cup + 2 tbsp **unsalted butter** at room temperature
3½ cups **confectioners' sugar**
1 tsp **vanilla bean paste**
⅔ cup **lemon curd** (available at gourmet supermarkets)
1–2 tbsp **milk**, if needed

For the decoration
½ cup **raspberry jam**
1½lb **white rolled fondant**
fuchsia and **mint green gel food colorings**
confectioners' sugar for dusting

A cake decorated to look like a present makes a fun birthday surprise. The cake and the decoration are simple to make yet the cake is striking in appearance with its lovely large bow. If you want to take the decoration a bit further you can use any leftover fondant to cut out dots, and then stick these to the cake to look like patterned wrapping paper.

1. Preheat the oven to 350°F, then grease and line an 8in square cake pan with parchment paper. In a medium bowl sift together the flour, baking powder, and salt, then set aside.

2. Put the butter, sugar, and lemon zest in a large bowl and, using an electric mixer, beat on medium-high speed until light and fluffy, about 5 minutes. Add the eggs, a little at a time, beating well between each addition. Once fully combined, add the flour mixture in three additions, mixing until just combined. If the batter feels a little stiff, add 1–2 tablespoons milk to lighten it.

3. Pour the batter into the prepared pan and gently level out. Bake for about 1¼ hours or until a skewer inserted into the center of the cake comes out clean. If the cake is browning too quickly, put a tent of foil over the top. Allow the cake to cool in the pan for 15 minutes before turning onto a wire rack to cool completely. If the cake is domed, use a serrated knife to level it.

4. To make the lemon syrup, put the sugar and lemon juice in a small pan and bring just to a boil, then gently simmer to dissolve the sugar. Remove from the heat and set aside until needed.

5. To make the buttercream, put the butter in a large bowl and, using an electric mixer, beat until lightened and smooth, about 3 minutes. Slowly add the confectioners' sugar to the butter, beating until incorporated, then beat on high speed for a few minutes until the buttercream is light and fluffy. Add the lemon curd and beat until combined. If the buttercream feels a little stiff, add 1–2 tablespoons milk to lighten it.

6. To assemble the cake, turn the cake upside down and slice into two even layers. Put the first cake layer (that was the top) onto a square cardboard cake board and brush the cake well with lemon syrup. Spread the jam evenly across the cake, leaving a ½–¾in border. Top with a layer of buttercream and then with the second layer of cake. Brush with more of the lemon syrup, and then cover the whole cake with the remaining buttercream. Allow the buttercream to set for 15 minutes before covering with the fondant.

7. Take two-thirds of the white fondant and knead it until pliable. The colder the fondant the longer it will need to be worked with to soften it. Dip a toothpick into the mint green coloring, add to the fondant, and knead until evenly combined. Dust the work surface with confectioners' sugar. Using a large rolling pin, roll the fondant into a square about ⅛in thick and large enough to cover the top and sides of the cake. The easiest way to do this is to take a piece of string and use it as a guide. Drape it over the cake and grip it where it meets the table. Lift the string from the cake and use this as a measure for your fondant.

8. Using the flats of your hands and arms to support the fondant, gently drape the fondant over the cake and smooth the top with your hands, applying a gentle pressure. Carefully work your way around the cake, gently smoothing the fondant onto the sides until you have a smooth square cake, trimming off the excess. Set the cake aside.

9. Take the remaining white fondant and knead it until pliable then add a small amount of fuschia coloring to the center and knead until evenly combined. Roll out the fondant into a long rectangle about ⅛in thick. Cut out three ribbons, two about 12in in length and 1¼in wide and one 10in in length and 1¼in wide. Take the longer ribbons and brush the underside with a little water, to act as a glue, then stick them to the cake to form a cross to look like a wrapped present.

10. To form the ribbon, cut the third length of fondant into two even pieces and fold them over to form two loops, pressing them to seal together. Take the ends of the loops and gently squeeze in the center to form a pleat. Using a little water, glue the ribbons together and then allow these loops to dry for at least 1 hour so that they hold their shape. Once dried, use a short length of fondant 1¼in wide to wrap around the center of the bow to cover the pleat, and then put the bow onto the cake. You can leave the bow as it is or you can add tails to the ribbon by cutting out two more short lengths, 1¼in wide, then cutting out a V-shape on both pieces and putting them under the bow.

Simple Celebration Chocolate Cake

SERVES 12

⅓ cup **cocoa powder**
3 tbsp strong hot **coffee**
3 tbsp hot **water**
1 cup + 6 tbsp **unsalted butter**
7oz **dark chocolate**
  (about 70% cocoa solids),
  finely chopped
1½ cups **light brown sugar**
4 large **eggs**
1⅓ cups **self-rising flour**
1 tsp **baking powder**

For the chocolate buttercream
3½oz **dark chocolate**
  (about 70% cocoa solids),
  finely chopped
¾ cup **unsalted butter**
  at room temperature
⅓ cup **heavy cream**
3¼ cups **confectioners' sugar**
a pinch of **salt**

For the decoration
18oz **white rolled fondant**
confectioners' sugar,
  for dusting
7oz **colored fondant**

I've made this easy, but richly flavored, cake to be a blank canvas for your decorative imagination. My version is made to look like a cake from a cartoon, but you can decorate it however you prefer.

1. Preheat the oven to 350°F, then grease and line two 8in cake pans with parchment paper, greasing the parchment too. Put the cocoa in a small bowl and pour in the coffee and hot water, whisking to form a smooth liquid. Set aside.

2. Put the butter and chocolate in a medium heatproof bowl set over a pan of gently simmering water, making sure the bottom of the bowl doesn't touch the water. Heat until fully melted, stirring frequently. Remove from the heat and set aside.

3. Whisk the sugar and eggs together until pale and thickened. Pour in the chocolate mixture and whisk to combine. Sift the flour and baking powder over the chocolate mixture and fold together until fully combined. Stir in the cocoa mixture. Divide the mixture equally between the two prepared pans and bake for 30 minutes or until the cakes spring back when lightly touched and a skewer inserted into the center comes out clean. Allow the cakes to cool in the pans for 10 minutes before turning onto a wire rack to cool completely.

4. To make the buttercream, melt the chocolate in a heatproof bowl set over a pan of gently simmering water, making sure the bottom of the bowl doesn't touch the water. Remove from the heat and let cool. Put the butter in a large bowl and, using an electric mixer, beat until light and creamy, about 3 minutes. Slowly pour in the cream, mixing until fully combined.

5. Add the confectioners' sugar, a little at a time. Once fully combined, add the salt and beat on high speed until the buttercream is light and fluffy. Pour in the cooled chocolate and mix until fully combined.

6. To assemble the cake, put the first cake layer onto a cardboard cake round or serving plate. If the cake is domed, use a serrated knife to level it. Top with a layer of the buttercream. Trim the second layer in the same way, if necessary, then place on top of the first. Cover the cake with the remaining buttercream. Put the cake in the fridge for 20–30 minutes before coating it with the fondant.

7. To decorate the cake, first create the white base layer. Take the white fondant and knead it until pliable. The colder the fondant the longer it will need to be worked with to soften it. Lightly dust the work surface with a little confectioners' sugar and then roll out the fondant into a circle large enough to cover the cake. The easiest way to do this is to take a piece of string and use it as a guide. Drape it over the cake and grip it where it meets the table. Lift the string from the cake and use this as a measure for your fondant. Using the flats of your hands and arms, gently drape the fondant over the cake, and use your hands to smooth the top, applying a gentle pressure. Carefully work your way around the cake, gently smoothing the fondant onto the sides, and trim off the excess.

8. To decorate the cake as I have done, take the colored fondant and roll it out into an 11in circle. Use a knife to cut out drip shapes all around the circle, making sure to leave the central 8in free of cuts. Lightly brush the cake with a little water and then drape the fondant over the cake. The water will act as a glue. Alternatively, you can decorate the cake in any way you want.

28

Red Velvet Cheesecake

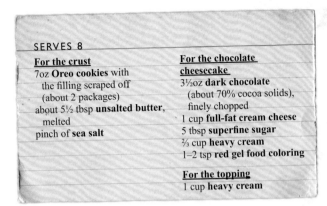

SERVES 8

For the crust
7oz **Oreo cookies** with
  the filling scraped off
  (about 2 packages)
about 5½ tbsp **unsalted butter,**
  melted
pinch of **sea salt**

For the chocolate cheesecake
3½oz **dark chocolate**
  (about 70% cocoa solids),
  finely chopped
1 cup **full-fat cream cheese**
5 tbsp **superfine sugar**
⅔ cup **heavy cream**
1–2 tsp **red gel food coloring**

For the topping
1 cup **heavy cream**

Red velvet cake is definitely a firm favorite and one of the most popular flavors at bakeries across the country, but how often have you seen it as a cheesecake? However, I had a hunch it could work and, even if I say so myself, the results are rather spectacular! Plus this no-bake recipe is a breeze to prepare. Try it and see.

1. Put the cookies in a medium bowl and, using the end of a rolling pin, crush them until fine. Add the butter and sea salt and mix well. Squeeze some of the mixture in your hand; it should stick together. If not, add a little extra butter. Pour the mixture into a 9in pie dish and press firmly over the bottom and sides. Put the pie dish in the fridge until needed.

2. To make the cheesecake, melt the chocolate in a heatproof bowl set over a pan of gently simmering water, making sure the bottom of the bowl doesn't touch the water. Remove from the heat and let cool.

3. Beat the cream cheese and sugar together in a medium bowl until smooth and creamy. In a medium bowl whisk together the cream and food coloring until the cream holds soft peaks. Pour in the melted chocolate and gently mix together. Add the cream mixture to the cream cheese mixture and fold together until evenly combined. Pour the mixture onto the prepared cookie crust and smooth out.

4. Chill for 2 hours or until set. Before serving, pour the heavy cream for the topping in a medium bowl and whisk until it holds soft peaks. Spread the cream over the top of the cheesecake.

Victoria Sponge

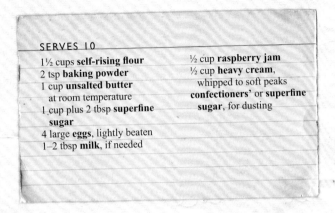

SERVES 10

1½ cups **self-rising flour**	½ cup **raspberry jam**
2 tsp **baking powder**	½ cup **heavy cream**,
1 cup **unsalted butter**	whipped to soft peaks
at room temperature	**confectioners'** or **superfine**
1 cup plus 2 tbsp **superfine**	**sugar**, for dusting
sugar	
4 large **eggs**, lightly beaten	
1–2 tbsp **milk**, if needed	

I was once asked what cake I would choose if I could eat only one type for the rest of my life, and unexpectedly I chose this: the humble Victoria Sponge. Although it is basic and very easy to make, there is something delicious about its simplicity. I don't know anyone who dislikes it—it really seems to have universal appeal.

1. Preheat the oven to 350°F, then lightly grease and line two 8in cake pans with parchment paper, greasing the parchment too.

2. In a medium bowl, whisk the flour and baking powder together to combine, then set aside.

3. Put the butter and sugar in a large bowl and, using an electric mixer, beat until light and fluffy, about 5 minutes. Add the eggs, a little at a time, beating until fully combined.

4. With the mixer on low, add the flour mixture in three additions until just combined. The cake batter should be a "dropping consistency," which means that if you take a spoonful of batter out of the bowl it should be light enough to fall easily from the spoon. If the batter is sticking to the spoon for too long, mix in 1–2 tablespoons milk to soften the batter.

5. Divide the cake batter evenly between the two prepared cake pans and gently level out. Bake for 25 minutes or until golden brown and coming away from the edge of the pan; a toothpick inserted into the center of a cake should come out clean. Let cool in the pan for 10 minutes before turning onto a wire rack to cool completely.

6. To assemble the cake, spread one layer of cake with the jam and top with the whipped cream. Sandwich together with the second layer of cake, and sprinkle with a little confectioners' or superfine sugar.

Meringues

MAKES 6	
⅔ cup **egg whites** (about 4 large eggs)	**For chocolate meringues** 1 tbsp **cocoa powder**
1½ cups **superfine sugar**	**For fruit meringues** ½oz **freeze-dried fruit,** crushed to a fine powder
For rose and pistachio meringues 1 tbsp **rose syrup** ⅓ cup **pistachio nuts,** finely chopped	

I love walking past bakeries that have piles of large meringues in the window. They look like soft pillowy clouds and they often have vibrant colors that just look so pretty. Making meringues is actually really easy and recreating the store-bought versions is very simple. You can make traditional white ones or flavor them.

1. Preheat the oven to 250°F and line a baking sheet with parchment paper.

2. Put the egg whites and sugar in a large, grease-free heatproof bowl set over a pan of gently simmering water, making sure the bottom of the bowl doesn't touch the water. Using an electric mixer, beat constantly until the sugar has dissolved and the egg mixture is just warm to the touch. The easiest way to test this is to dip your thumb and forefinger into the mixture and rub them together; if you can feel sugar, continue beating a little longer. Remove from the heat and beat the meringue until stiff and glossy.

3. If you want to make flavored meringues, fold in any of the suggested options, leaving a little of the flavoring to sprinkle on top of the meringues before baking.

4. For plain or flavored meringues, using a large metal spoon, place 6 large dollops of the meringue onto the prepared baking sheet about an inch apart from each other. Sprinkle over a little of the flavorings, if using. Bake for 1½ hours, then turn off the heat and allow the meringues to cool completely in the oven.

Mix & Match Cupcakes

What better to way to entertain a party full of kids than a cupcake-decorating session?
Have everything ready to go and let the kids go wild and decorate the cakes as they prefer.

MAKES 12

Vanilla cupcakes
1¼ cups **all-purpose flour**
2¼ tsp **baking powder**
¼ tsp **salt**
½ cup **unsalted butter**,
    at room temperature
1 cup **superfine sugar**
2 large **eggs**, lightly beaten
1 tsp **vanilla extract**
⅔ cup **buttermilk**

MAKES 12

Chocolate cupcakes
½ cup **cocoa powder**
½ cup boiling **water**
⅓ cup **buttermilk**
3 tbsp **vegetable oil**
¾ cup plus 1 tbsp **light
   brown sugar**
1 tsp **vanilla extract**
1 large **egg**
1 large **egg yolk**

1 cup **all-purpose flour**
1 tsp **baking soda**
¼ tsp **salt**

1. Preheat the oven to 350°F and line a standard 12-cup muffin pan with paper liners. In a medium bowl whisk the flour, baking powder, and salt together to combine, then set aside.

2. Put the butter and sugar in a large bowl and, using an electric mixer, beat until light and fluffy, about 5 minutes. Add the eggs and vanilla extract a little at a time, beating until fully combined.

3. Add the flour mixture in three additions, alternating with the buttermilk, starting and finishing with the flour mixture. Divide the batter among the prepared muffin cups, filling each liner about half-full. Bake for 22–25 minutes or until a toothpick inserted into the center of a cake comes out clean.

1. Preheat the oven to 350°F and line a standard 12-cup muffin pan with paper liners.

2. Put the cocoa powder and boiling water in a large bowl and mix until the cocoa is fully dissolved.

3. Add the buttermilk, oil, light brown sugar, and vanilla extract and mix to combine.

4. Mix in the egg and egg yolk, then add the flour, baking soda, and salt, and mix until just combined.

5. Divide the batter between the muffin cups filling each liner about half-full. Bake for 15–18 minutes or until a toothpick inserted into the center of a cake comes out clean.

34

Italian meringue buttercream
¾ cup **superfine sugar**
3 large **egg whites** .
1 cup + 3 tbsp **unsalted butter**,
 at room temperature

1. To make the buttercream, put ⅓ cup water and the sugar in a pan over medium heat. Bring to a boil and have a sugar thermometer ready.

2. Meanwhile, pour the egg whites into a clean, grease-free bowl (this is best done using a freestanding electric mixer). Start beating the whites on high speed when the syrup in the pan reaches about 240°F on the sugar thermometer. Cook until the syrup registers 250°F. With the mixer still running, pour the syrup in a slow stream down the side of the bowl containing the whites, avoiding the beaters. Continue beating on high speed until the meringue is at room temperature.

3. With the mixer on medium-high speed, add the butter, a few pieces at a time, beating until fully combined. When adding the butter it can sometimes look curdled; if this happens don't worry, just keep mixing and eventually it will smooth out again forming a light buttercream.

4. Flavorings: once the buttercream is made you could add 3½oz dark chocolate (about 70% cocoa solids), melted and cooled, or ½ cup raspberry jam or lemon curd, if you like.

Classic vanilla buttercream
1 cup + 1 tbsp **unsalted
  butter**, at room temperature
2 tsp **vanilla bean paste**
⅓ cup **heavy cream**
4½ cups **confectioners' sugar**,
  sifted
a pinch of **salt**

Whipped ganache frosting
7oz **dark chocolate**
  (about 70% cocoa solids),
  finely chopped
¾ cup plus 1 tbsp **heavy cream**

1. Beat the butter and vanilla paste using an electric mixer until light and creamy. With the mixer on medium speed, slowly incorporate the heavy cream. Once light and smooth, slowly incorporate the confectioners' sugar and salt, and then beat on high speed until light and fluffy.

2. Flavorings: I prefer this classic buttercream as it is, but you could mix in ½ cup lemon curd after adding the confectioners' sugar, if you like, or flavor it with melted chocolate or raspberry jam as for the Italian meringue buttercream.

1. Put the chocolate in a large heatproof bowl and set aside. Put the cream in a small pan over medium heat and bring just to a boil. Pour in the chocolate and let stand for 2 minutes before gently stirring together to form a silky smooth ganache. Cool in the fridge for a few minutes until it just begins to thicken. It should be shiny and pourable, looking a little like thick custard. Whisk in short bursts until the mixture is just holding its shape.

2. This frosting isn't easy to pipe because it will easily melt when held in a piping bag, so I prefer to use an offset spatula to apply it.

Chocolate & Amaretto Baked Alaska

SERVES 6	For the amaretto Swiss
butter, for greasing	**meringue**
4 large **eggs**	⅓ cup **egg whites** (about
½ cup **superfine sugar**	2 large eggs)
½ cup **all-purpose flour**	1 cup **superfine sugar**
½ cup **cocoa powder**	¼ tsp **cream of tartar**
1⅔ cups **chocolate**	2 tbsp **amaretto**
ice cream, softened	

For the amaretto syrup
¼ cup **superfine sugar**
2–3 tbsp **amaretto**

The combination of chocolate and amaretto is one of my favorites, and when used in a baked Alaska it turns an old-fashioned dessert into something completely different. Although there are a few more steps of preparation than is usual for a basic baked Alaska, this version is so much more rewarding both in looks and, of course, in taste.

1. Preheat the oven to 350°F, then grease a 10 × 15in high-sided baking sheet and line with parchment paper, greasing the parchment too. Put the eggs and sugar in a heatproof bowl set over a pan of gently simmering water, making sure the bowl doesn't touch the water. Whisk constantly until the sugar has dissolved and the mixture is just warm to the touch.

2. Remove the bowl from the pan and, using an electric mixer, beat for 5 minutes on high speed, then reduce the speed to medium and beat for another 3 minutes. By this stage the mixture should have tripled in volume, and when the beaters are lifted from the bowl they should form a slowly dissolving ribbon.

3. Sift in the flour and cocoa powder, and gently fold together, making sure all the dry ingredients are combined but trying to keep as much volume as possible. Pour the batter into the prepared pan and very gently level it out. Bake for 15 minutes or until the cake is risen and a skewer inserted into the center of the cake comes out clean. Let cool in the pan for 10 minutes before turning onto a wire rack to cool completely.

4. To make the syrup, put 3 tablespoons water and the sugar in a small pan and bring to a boil, then simmer for about 2 minutes or until the sugar is fully dissolved. Remove from the heat and add the amaretto to taste. Take a 1-quart (7in wide) bowl and line with a piece of plastic wrap, leaving a large overhang.

5. Cut out two discs of cake, one to fit the top and one to fit the bottom of the bowl, and use the remaining cake to cut out a strip to line the sides of the bowl. Line the bowl with the bottom and side cake pieces and brush liberally with the syrup.

6. Fill with the ice cream and put the larger cake disc on top, then press firmly to seal. Fold over the plastic wrap and freeze for about 1 hour or until the ice cream is firm.

7. To assemble the dessert, put the egg whites, sugar, and cream of tartar for the amaretto Swiss meringue into a grease-free heatproof bowl set over a pan of gently simmering water. Using an electric mixer, beat constantly until the sugar has dissolved. Remove the bowl from the heat and beat until the meringue forms stiff, glossy peaks. Add the amaretto and beat to combine.

8. Remove the ice cream-filled cake from the freezer and unwrap, then turn onto a serving plate. Pour the meringue onto the cake and spread evenly to cover completely. Use a kitchen blowtorch to brown the meringue, or brown it in a preheated 450°F oven for 3–4 minutes.

TIP

If you want to make this a spectacular finish to a meal, you can take a small pan with 2 tbsp amaretto and gently warm it over low heat. Once ready to serve, light the amaretto and pour it over the Baked Alaska.

36

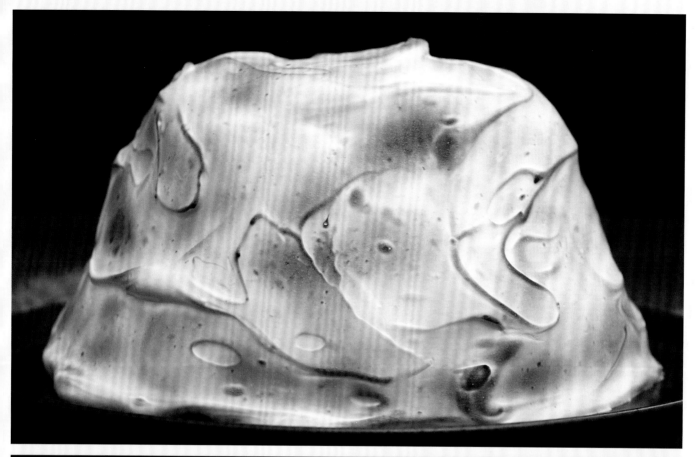
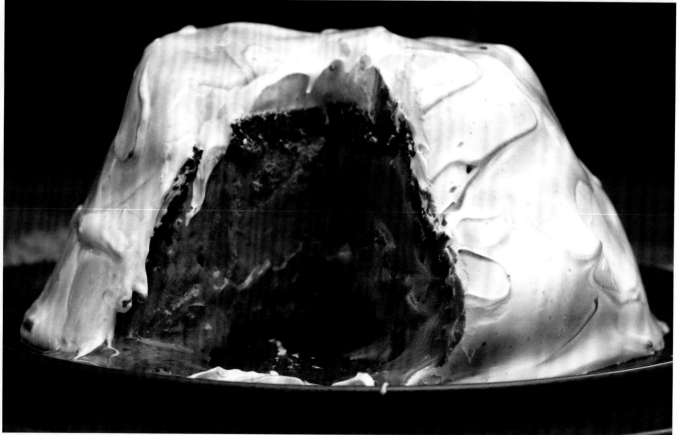

Fresh Blueberry Marshmallows

MAKES ABOUT 45

oil spray, for greasing
2 cups + 2 tbsp **superfine sugar**
1 tbsp **liquid glucose.**
8 sheets of **gelatin**
2 large **egg whites**
1 cup **blueberries**

For the coating
⅓ cup **confectioners' sugar**
⅓ cup **cornstarch**

You may think that it is difficult to make marshmallows, but that couldn't be further from the truth. If you can make a meringue, you can make marshmallows. These are pillowy soft and they melt in your mouth. To counteract the sweetness, I have added some fresh blueberries, which pop in your mouth as you eat the marshmallows—absolutely delicious!

1. Lightly grease a 9 × 13in high-sided baking sheet or brownie pan, then line with a piece of plastic wrap and lightly grease the plastic wrap. To make the coating, mix the confectioners' sugar and cornstarch together and dust the plastic wrap with a thin layer of this mixture, reserving the remainder.

2. Put the sugar, glucose and ⅓ cup water in a medium pan over medium heat. Bring to a boil and have a sugar thermometer ready.

3. Meanwhile, put the gelatin in a medium bowl and cover with ½ cup cold water.

4. Also, pour the egg whites into a clean, grease-free bowl (this is best done using a freestanding electric mixer). Start beating the whites on high speed to form soft peaks when the syrup in the pan reaches about 240°F on the sugar thermometer. Cook until the syrup registers 245°F. With the mixer still running, pour the syrup in a slow stream down the side of the bowl containing the whites, avoiding the beaters.

5. Put the softened gelatin and the water in the now empty syrup pan over low heat, then stir until the gelatin is fully melted. Pour this mixture into the meringue mixture and continue whisking until the mixture is cool.

6. Pour half this marshmallow mixture into the prepared pan and, using a greased spatula, spread into an even layer. Sprinkle in the blueberries and then top with the remaining marshmallow. Sprinkle the top of the marshmallow with a thin layer of the coating and then allow to set at room temperature for a few hours.

7. Once fully set, transfer the marshmallow to a sheet of parchment paper and cut into squares using either a pizza cutter or scissors. Roll the marshmallows in the remaining coating and then shake off the excess.

8. Store in a sealed container; the marshmallows will keep for a few days (but without the blueberries they will keep for at least a week).

Jelly and Custard Cups

MAKES 6

1¼lb mixed **summer fruits**
(such as **strawberries,
raspberries, blackberries,
blackcurrants,** and
redcurrants)
4 tbsp **superfine sugar**
about ⅓ cup **water or prosecco**
4 sheets of **gelatin**
confectioners' sugar, for dusting

For the custard
1 **vanilla bean**
1⅔ cups **whole milk**
3 tbsp **superfine sugar**
2 tbsp **cornstarch**
4 large **egg yolks**

This dessert is firmly rooted in my childhood, like many of my ideas. I remember eating a lot of jelly as a child, at home, at school, and at parties when I was little. Although there is nothing wrong with a simple and classic jelly, these look a little more refined, and if you make them with prosecco (not for the kids, of course), they have a very adult twist.

1. Put 1lb mixed summer fruits, the sugar, and ⅓ cup water or prosecco in a large pan over medium heat. Cook gently, stirring occasionally, until the fruit has softened and released a lot of its juice. Strain the fruit through a sieve into a glass measuring cup, setting the softened fruit aside (it isn't needed for the recipe but would be great served with some ice cream). You will need 1⅓ cups of liquid, so top off as needed with water or prosecco.

2. Put the gelatin in a small pan and pour in a little of the fruit juice, just enough to cover the gelatin. Allow this mixture to soften for 10 minutes, then place over low heat and stir until the gelatin is fully dissolved. Pour this mixture back into the remaining fruit juice and stir to combine. Divide the jelly mixture among six small glasses and chill for 4–6 hours until fully set.

3. To make the custard, scrape the seeds from the vanilla bean, then put the bean and seeds in a medium pan with the milk. Bring to a boil, then simmer over medium heat.

4. Whisk the sugar and cornstarch together in a medium heatproof bowl. Add the egg yolks and whisk together until pale and thickened.

5. Remove the vanilla bean from the milk, and then pour half the hot milk over the eggs, whisking constantly. Pour back into the pan and cook over medium heat, whisking constantly until it thickens. Pour into a bowl and let cool slightly, then divide among the six glasses. Chill until ready to serve. To serve, top each glass with a little of the remaining fresh fruit and a light dusting of confectioners' sugar.

MY SISTER AND BROTHER, NICOLA AND NEIL

Praline Profiterole Tower

SERVES 8

⅔ cup **all-purpose flour**	6 large **egg yolks**
4 tbsp **unsalted butter**	¼ cup **superfine sugar**
¼ tsp **superfine sugar**	4 tbsp **all-purpose flour**
¼ tsp **salt**	2 tsp **vanilla extract**
2–3 large **eggs**	
	For the chocolate sauce
For the hazelnut praline	3oz **dark chocolate**
¾ cup skinned **hazelnuts**	(about 70% cocoa solids),
½ cup **superfine sugar**	finely chopped
	2 tsp **unsalted butter**
For the pastry cream	1 tbsp **honey**
1¾ cups **whole milk**	½ cup **heavy cream**

I know profiteroles are a bit retro, but I love them. There is nothing wrong with choux pastry, cream, and chocolate—it's a classic for a reason. For a more modern version, I fill the buns with pastry cream mixed with hazelnut praline; they are richer than the classic so the portion sizes should be smaller. To sterilize the jars for the praline paste, run through the dishwasher.

1. To make the hazelnut praline, preheat the oven to 400°F. Put the hazelnuts on a baking sheet lined with parchment paper and place into the hot oven for 5 minutes or until fragrant. Remove from the oven and let cool. Put the sugar in a medium pan over medium heat and allow to dissolve and cook until dark golden brown in color, stopping before it starts to smoke.

2. Immediately pour the caramel carefully over the hazelnuts, then let cool. Break into pieces and put in the bowl of a food processor. Pulse to break the pieces into smaller chunks, then process until you have a smooth paste; this will take a few minutes. Put the praline paste in a sterilized jar. (This can be prepared days ahead, as it keeps very well.)

3. To make the pastry cream, put the milk in a large pan over medium heat and bring to a boil. Meanwhile, in a medium bowl, whisk the egg yolks, sugar, flour, and vanilla extract until pale and smooth. Pour in half of the hot milk and whisk to combine. Pour the egg mixture back into the pan and put back on the heat. Bring to a boil, whisking constantly, until thickened. Pour the pastry cream into a bowl and press a piece of plastic wrap onto the surface to keep a skin from forming. Cool and chill.

4. For the choux buns, line two baking sheets with parchment paper. Sift the flour onto a sheet of waxed paper. Put the butter, sugar, salt, and ½ cup water in a medium pan over medium-high heat and bring to a rolling boil. Take off the heat and pour in the flour. Using a wooden spoon, beat to combine. Put back on the heat and beat the dough for a few minutes or until the dough comes away from the sides of the pan.

5. Transfer the dough to a medium bowl and beat vigorously until no longer steaming. Beat in the eggs, one at a time—you may not need them all; check the consistency of the dough after each addition. It should be smooth and shiny and will fall from the wooden spoon forming a V-shaped ribbon. If it looks almost right after 2 eggs, just add a little of the third and test again. Put the dough in a piping bag fitted with a plain piping tip and pipe into rounds on the prepared baking sheet about 1in in diameter. Using a finger dipped in water, gently tap any peaks down.

6. Bake for 20–25 minutes or until risen and golden brown. Remove the pan from the oven and, using a sharp knife, make a hole in the bottom of each choux bun. Turn the oven off and put the choux buns back into the oven, bottom up, for 10 minutes; this will help keep the buns crisp.

7. To fill the buns, take the pastry cream out of the fridge and beat in the praline paste. Put the praline cream in a piping bag fitted with a small plain piping tip and fill each bun with cream.

8. To make the chocolate sauce, put the chocolate, butter, honey, and cream in a small pan and cook over medium heat, stirring occasionally, until the chocolate melts and the sauce is smooth and fully combined. Pour into a bowl and let cool slightly. The longer you leave the sauce the thicker it will become. To thin it out, gently heat it up until the desired consistency. To serve the profiteroles, take a large plate and pile the choux buns in the middle. Drizzle over the warm chocolate sauce, and then dig in!

Zuccotto Summer Pudding

SERVES 8–10

2 tbsp **unsalted butter**, melted and cooled, plus extra butter for greasing
4 large **eggs**
½ cup **superfine sugar**
¾ cup **all-purpose flour**
heavy cream, to serve (optional)

For the fruit filling
1¼lb **summer fruits** (such as **strawberries, raspberries, blueberries, redcurrants, blackberries, and cherries**)
⅔ cup **superfine sugar**
2 tbsp **crème de cassis**

For the cream filling
1 cup **heavy cream**
1 tbsp **confectioners' sugar**
1 tsp **vanilla bean paste**

Summer pudding is a stalwart of British cooking. Normally made with stale bread, it is a classic that is very easy to put together. My version crosses the British classic with an Italian classic, zuccotto, which is similar in presentation except that it is a cake filled with a cream or ice cream mixture. My dessert combines the best of both worlds.

1. Preheat the oven to 350°F, then line a 10 × 15in high-sided baking sheet with parchment paper, greasing the parchment too. Put the eggs and sugar in a heatproof bowl set over a pan of gently simmering water, making sure the bottom of the bowl doesn't touch the water. Whisk constantly until the sugar has dissolved and the mixture is just warm to the touch.

2. Remove from the heat and, using an electric mixer, beat for 5 minutes on high speed, then reduce the speed to medium and beat for another 3 minutes. By this stage the mixture should have tripled in volume, and when the beaters are lifted from the bowl they should form a slowly dissolving ribbon.

3. Sift in the flour and gently fold together making sure all the ingredients are combined but trying to keep as much volume as possible. Take a large spoonful of the batter and add to the melted butter, then mix together (this will lighten the butter and help to incorporate it into the batter). Gently fold this into the batter.

4. Pour the batter into the prepared pan and very gently level out. Bake for 15 minutes or until the cake is risen; a skewer inserted into the center of the cake should come out clean. Let cool in the pan for 10 minutes before turning onto a wire rack to cool completely.

5. To make the filling, put all the ingredients in a medium pan and cook over medium heat until the fruit has softened slightly and there is a vibrant syrup in the bottom of the pan. Drain the fruit and set aside, reserving the syrup.

6. To make the cream filling, whisk all the ingredients together until the cream holds stiff peaks. To assemble the pudding, line a 1-quart bowl with plastic wrap, making sure there is an overhang to help remove the pudding later. Cut out two discs of cake, one to fit the bottom of the bowl and one to fit the top. Cut the remaining cake into thin strips.

7. Dip all the cake into the reserved syrup and use all but the top piece to line the prepared bowl. Spread the cream filling across the bottom and up the sides of the bowl, covering all the cake. Pour the fruit into the bowl and seal with the larger disc of cake. Press a piece of plastic wrap to the top of the pudding and put a small plate on top. Put a weight, such as a can of beans, onto the plate to weight it down. This helps to seal the pudding so that it holds its shape. Chill for 4–5 hours before serving.

8. Remove the weight and plate, and turn the bowl over onto a serving plate. Use the overhang of plastic wrap to tease the pudding from the bowl. Serve on its own or with a little extra cream.

Love Heart Cookies

MAKES ABOUT 30

3 cups **all-purpose flour**,
  plus extra for dusting
½ tsp **salt**
1 cup **superfine sugar**
1 cup **unsalted butter**, diced
  and chilled
1 large **egg**
1 large **egg yolk**
1 tsp **vanilla bean paste**

For the decoration
1½lb **white fondant**
red gel food coloring
2 cups **confectioners' sugar**,
  plus extra for dusting

Love heart sweets, or candy hearts, might just taste of sugar, but they are undeniably cute. I remember passing them around in my early school days, when it was very important that you chose your message carefully. Why not bake these cookies based on the childhood sweets and use them as a fun and personal favor for a wedding? You can tailor the message to whatever you like, be it the wedding couple's names or simply words of love.

1. Line two baking sheets with parchment paper. Put the flour, salt, and sugar in the bowl of a food processor and pulse to combine. Add the butter and pulse until the mixture resembles coarse bread crumbs. (Alternatively, rub the butter into the flour mixture by hand until it resembles coarse bread crumbs.) Add the egg, yolk, and vanilla paste and pulse (or stir) until the mixture just comes together. Transfer to a lightly floured work surface and gently knead together until uniform. Divide the dough in half and wrap in plastic wrap, then chill for about 1 hour.

2. Working with one half of the dough at a time, roll out to a thickness of ¼in. Cut out rounds using a 3½in cookie cutter. Re-roll the scraps to cut out more cookies. Lift the cookies off the surface with a metal spatula and put them onto the prepared baking sheets, then chill for 15–20 minutes. Preheat the oven to 350°F.

3. Bake for 13–15 minutes or until the edges turn golden. Let cool on the baking sheets for 10 minutes before transferring to a wire rack to cool completely.

4. To decorate, take the fondant and knead it until pliable. Knead a few drops of red food coloring into the fondant to make it light pink. Wrap the fondant in plastic wrap while you make the icing. Sift the confectioners' sugar into a medium bowl and add 2 tablespoons of water. Beat with a wooden spoon until combined. Using a toothpick, add a little coloring to make the royal icing red. The royal icing should be barely pourable, so if it's too thin, add a little extra confectioners' sugar; if it's too thick, add a little more water.

5. Roll out the fondant on a work surface dusted with a little confectioners' sugar until it is about ⅛in thick. Cut out 3½in rounds with the cookie cutter. Put the royal icing in a piping bag fitted with a thin round (about ⅛in) piping tip and pipe a swirl of icing onto each cookie. Put the rounds of fondant onto the cookies. Use the remaining royal icing to pipe the decoration: first pipe a circle around the outside edge of the cookie, and then pipe a heart in the center. To replicate the look of the love heart sweets, you can then pipe words and phrases inside the heart.

Flourless Chocolate & Blackberry Cake

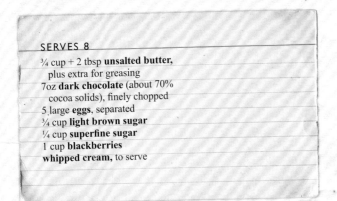

SERVES 8

¾ cup + 2 tbsp **unsalted butter,**
   plus extra for greasing
7oz **dark chocolate** (about 70%
   cocoa solids), finely chopped
5 large **eggs,** separated
¾ cup **light brown sugar**
¼ cup **superfine sugar**
1 cup **blackberries**
whipped cream, to serve

Everyone knows that chocolate is the ultimate romantic food, and this cake is pure romance. A gooey warm flourless cake studded with little bursts of blackberry—it's the perfect dish to make for a date or Valentine's dinner. It will most definitely impress.

1. Preheat the oven to 350°F, then line the bottom of a 9in springform cake pan with parchment paper, greasing the parchment too. Set a heatproof bowl over a pan of lightly simmering water, making sure the bottom of the bowl doesn't touch the water. Add the chocolate and butter to the bowl and let melt, stirring occasionally.

2. In a medium bowl, whisk the egg yolks and light brown sugar together until thickened and pale. Put the egg whites into a clean, grease-free bowl and whisk until they form firm peaks, then slowly pour in the superfine sugar and whisk until the meringue is stiff and glossy.

3. Whisk the chocolate mixture into the egg yolk mixture, then stir in a third of the meringue to lighten the batter. Gently fold in the remaining meringue, trying to knock out as little air as possible.

4. Pour the batter into the prepared pan and gently level out. Sprinkle in the blackberries and bake for 35 to 40 minutes or until the cake is risen and has thin cracks on top. Let the cake cool in the pan for 10 minutes before removing the springform collar and cooling on a wire rack.

5. When warm, this cake is very light and melts on the tongue. If you prefer a slightly firmer texture, let the cake cool completely and then pop it into the fridge; served cold it will have a slightly brownie-type texture. Serve with a little whipped cream.

Rose & Raspberry Cheesecake

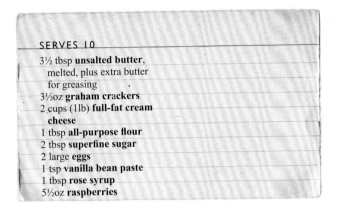

SERVES 10

3½ tbsp **unsalted butter**,
  melted, plus extra butter
  for greasing
3½oz **graham crackers**
2 cups (1lb) **full-fat cream
  cheese**
1 tbsp **all-purpose flour**
2 tbsp **superfine sugar**
2 large **eggs**
1 tsp **vanilla bean paste**
1 tbsp **rose syrup**
5½oz **raspberries**

A rose for a romantic occasion is traditional and classic, so why mess with a classic? Adding the rose syrup and raspberry to this cheesecake cuts the richness and adds a delicate floral note that is definitely not soapy or overpowering.

1. Preheat the oven to 350°F, then grease and line an 8in springform cake pan with parchment paper. Put the graham crackers in a medium bowl and, using the base of a rolling pin, crush them into fine crumbs. Add the melted butter and stir to coat evenly.

2. Firmly press the mixture into the bottom of the prepared pan. Bake for 10 minutes, or until the edges turn golden, then remove from the oven and let cool while you make the filling. Reduce the oven to 300°F.

3. Put the cream cheese and flour in a large bowl and, using an electric mixer, beat until smooth. Add the sugar and beat until just combined—the less you beat a baked cheesecake mixture the better; if you over-beat, the cake will have a higher chance of developing cracks.

4. Lightly beat the eggs and vanilla paste together and slowly incorporate this mixture into the cream cheese mixture, beating until just fully combined. Pour about a quarter of the mixture into another bowl and stir in the rose syrup.

5. Add the raspberries to the larger portion of mixture and pour onto the prepared crust, then gently smooth out. Add the rose-flavored mixture on top and, using a knife, swirl gently into the vanilla mixture. Bake for 1 hour or until the edges are set but the center is still wobbly. Cool and chill overnight before serving. This firms up the cheesecake and gives it a delicious silky-smooth texture.

49

Concorde

SERVES 10

6 large **egg whites**
⅓ cup **superfine sugar**
2½ cups **confectioners' sugar**
⅓ cup **cocoa powder**
confectioners' sugar or **cocoa powder**, for dusting

For the simple chocolate mousse
6½oz **dark chocolate** (about 70% cocoa solids), finely chopped
about 2 cups **heavy cream**

This cake is beautiful and looks so much more complicated to make than it actually is. If you have made meringues before, you will be fine—but if you haven't, don't worry, because it really is very simple. This is my version of a cake created by the famous Parisian chef Gaston Lenôtre in 1969 to celebrate the inaugural flight of the Concorde.

1. Preheat the oven to 225°F and line three baking sheets with parchment paper. Using an 8in cake pan as a template, draw a circle on each piece of parchment, then turn it over so that the drawing is underneath.

2. Put the egg whites into a clean, grease-free bowl and, using an electric mixer, beat until they form stiff peaks. Slowly pour in the superfine sugar and beat until the meringue is stiff and glossy. Sift the confectioners' sugar and cocoa powder over the meringue and gently fold together, being as gentle as possible.

3. Spoon the meringue into a piping bag fitted with a ½in wide plain piping tip and pipe three discs on the parchment paper using the drawn templates, piping in a spiral starting at the center and working outward. Using the remaining meringue, pipe long strips onto the prepared baking sheets alongside the discs. Bake for about 1 hour 40 minutes or until firm and crisp. Turn off the oven and allow the meringues to cool in the oven for 2 hours.

4. To make the mousse, melt the chocolate in a large heatproof bowl set over a pan of gently simmering water, making sure the bottom of the bowl doesn't touch the water. Remove from the heat and let cool. Whisk the cream to soft peaks then pour it into the bowl with the chocolate and whisk to combine. The resulting mousse should be fairly thick and be able to hold its shape, but not so thick it can't be spread easily. If it is too thick and looks overwhipped, pour in a little extra cream or milk and stir to loosen the mousse.

5. To assemble the cake, use a little of the mousse to stick the first meringue disc to a cardboard cake board or serving plate. Spread about a third of the mousse over the meringue and then add another meringue and repeat the process. Top with the final meringue and then coat the top and sides of the cake with the remaining third of the mousse.

6. To finish the decoration, use a serrated knife to gently cut the meringue strips into pieces. Lightly press these all over the cake and lightly dust with either confectioners' sugar or cocoa powder. You can either serve the cake now or you can freeze it for a few hours; this will soften the meringue slightly. If you do freeze the cake, thaw it in the fridge for a few hours before serving.

TIP

Use a gentle sawing motion when cutting the meringue, as it is very fragile and breaks easily.

Traditional Wedding Cake

SERVES 125

For the large (12in) tier
3 cups **golden raisins**
4 cups **currants**
3 cups **raisins**
½lb **mixed candied peel**
8oz **candied cherries**,
  roughly chopped
zest of 2 **oranges**
zest of 2 **lemons**
½ cup **brandy**

2 cups **unsalted butter**
  at room temperature,
  plus extra for greasing
3¼ cups **all-purpose flour**
2⅓ cups **almond flour**
1 tsp **salt**
2 tsp **ground cinnamon**
2 tsp **pumpkin pie spice**
2¼ cups **superfine sugar**
10 large **eggs**

For the medium (9in) tier
1½ cups **golden raisins**
2 cups **currants**
1½ cups **raisins**
4oz **mixed candied peel**
4oz **candied cherries**,
  roughly chopped
zest of 1 **orange**
zest of 1 **lemon**
¼ cup **brandy**

1 cup **unsalted butter**
  at room temperature,
  plus extra for greasing
1⅔ cups **all-purpose flour**
1¼ cups **almond flour**
½ tsp **salt**
1½ tsp **ground cinnamon**
1½ tsp **pumpkin pie spice**
1 cup + 2 tbsp **superfine sugar**
5 large **eggs**

For the small (6in) tier
¾ cup **golden raisins**
1 cup **currants**
¾ cup **raisins**
2oz **mixed candied peel**
2oz **candied cherries**,
  roughly chopped
zest of ½ **orange**
zest of ½ **lemon**
2 tbsp **brandy**

½ cup **unsalted butter**
  at room temperature,
  plus extra for greasing
¾ cup plus 2 tbsp **all-purpose
  flour**
⅔ cup **almond flour**
¼ tsp **salt**
1 tsp **ground cinnamon**
1 tsp **pumpkin pie spice**
½ cup + 1 tbsp **superfine sugar**

This wedding cake is an absolute classic. It is based on my Nanna's recipe, and my family believes it may have even been the recipe that was used for her own wedding during the Second World War. Because all the ingredients were rationed at the time, her friends and neighbors pooled their ration coupons so that they were able to get enough ingredients together to make the cake for her special day. The cakes take a long time to bake, but fruit cake keeps very well, so you can spread the work over a number of days, or even weeks. If preparing the cakes ahead, wrap them well in plastic wrap and store until ready to decorate.

For the decoration	**Materials**
12oz jar **apricot jam**, sieved	12in, 9in, and 6in
confectioners' sugar, for dusting	cardboard cake rounds
7¾lb **marzipan**	wooden or plastic dowel rods
7¾lb **white fondant**	14in cardboard cake
2¼lb **pale-brown fondant**	drum (optional)
2¼lb **teal blue fondant**	chocolate-brown ribbon

1. The night before you want to make the large cake, put the fruits, zests, and brandy into a large bowl and mix together. Cover with plastic wrap and let soak overnight.

2. The next day, preheat the oven to 325°F, then grease and triple-line a deep 12in round cake pan with parchment paper. In a medium bowl whisk the flour, almonds, salt, and spices together to combine, then set aside

3. Put the butter and sugar in a large bowl and, using an electric mixer, beat until light and fluffy, about 5 minutes. Beat in the eggs, a little at a time, beating until fully combined. With the mixer on low, add the flour mixture, a large spoonful at a time, mixing just until combined. Using a large spatula or metal spoon, fold in the fruit.

4. Scrape the batter into the prepared pan and bake for 4 hours or until a toothpick inserted into the center comes out clean. If the cake is browning too quickly, put a tent of foil over the top. Allow the cake to cool completely in the pan before removing.

5. Repeat the process for the other layers, baking the 9in cake for 3 hours and the 6in cake for 2 hours.

6. To decorate the cakes you need the tops to have a level surface; if the cakes are domed, use a serrated knife to trim them level. Turn the cakes upside down onto the cake boards so that you have the perfect base as the top: put the medium and small cakes onto their respective cake rounds and the large cake onto the cake drum. Put the apricot jam into a small pan and heat gently to melt. Brush the large cake with a thin layer of the jam, which will act as a glue for the marzipan.

7. Dust the work surface lightly with confectioners' sugar, then roll out 4lb of the marzipan until it is large enough to cover the top and sides of the large cake. The easiest way to do this is to take a piece of string and use it as a guide. Drape it over the cake and grip it where it meets the table. Lift the string from the cake and use this as a measure for your marzipan. Using the flats of your hands and arms, gently drape the marzipan onto the cake, smoothing it carefully down the sides of the cake. Use a knife to trim off any excess. Allow the marzipan to dry out for a day before covering in fondant.

8. Take 4lb of the white fondant and knead it until pliable. The colder the fondant the longer it will need to be worked with to soften it. Dust a work surface lightly with confectioners' sugar. Roll out the fondant until it is large enough to cover the top and sides of the cake. Brush the marzipan with a little water to create a slightly sticky surface. Using the flats of your hands and arms, gently drape the fondant over the cake, and use your hands to smooth the top, applying a gentle pressure. Carefully work your way around the cake, gently smoothing the fondant onto the sides, and trim off the excess.

9. Repeat this process with the other two cakes using 2¼lb of fondant and marzipan for the 9in cake and 1½lb of both for the 6in cake.

10. For the decoration, take the chocolate-brown fondant and roll it until ¹⁄₁₆in thick, then cut out as many strips as possible, in different widths ¾–1½in wide. Repeat with the teal blue fondant. You now need to "glue" these strips to all three cakes. I like to attach them in a random fashion, so that the cake doesn't look symmetrical. For the two largest tiers, cut the strips into lengths that are long enough to go up the sides of the cake and about 2in toward the center, but not all the way. For the top tier, the strips need to be long enough to cover the cake, as the top will be visible. To attach the strips, brush them lightly with a little water and press the wet sides to the cakes. Allow these to dry and adhere onto the cake for a few hours before assembling the cake.

11. When ready to assemble, push four dowel rods into the 12in cake about 2in in from the outside edge, then mark where they are flush with the fondant. Now remove the dowels and cut them to fit, then push them back inside the cake. Repeat the process with the 9in cake. These dowels will act as a support so that the cakes won't sink into each other when stacked.

12. Transport the cakes as separate layers. To assemble, put the large cake onto a large cake stand or a cardboard cake drum and center the medium cake on top followed by the small cake. To finish the decoration, put a strip of ribbon around the bottom of each cake, using double-sided sticky tape to secure the seam. I also like to top the cake with a few flowers, preferably the same ones used in the wedding.

FAMILY WEDDING

CHAPTER TWO: ROMANCE

Neapolitan Wedding Cake

SERVES 50

For the large (9in) vanilla cake
butter or **oil**, for greasing
6 large **eggs**
¾ cup **superfine sugar**
2 tsp **vanilla bean paste**
1 cup plus 1 tbsp **all-purpose flour**

For the large (9in) chocolate cake
6 large **eggs**
¾ cup **superfine sugar**
2 tsp **vanilla bean paste**
¾ cup **all-purpose flour**
⅔ cup **cocoa powder**

For the small (6in) vanilla cake
3 large **eggs**
⅓ cup **superfine sugar**
1 tsp **vanilla bean paste**
½ cup **all-purpose flour**

For the small (6in) chocolate cake
3 large **eggs**
6 tbsp **superfine sugar**
1 tsp **vanilla bean paste**
⅓ cup **all-purpose flour**
⅓ cup **cocoa powder**

For the strawberry buttercream
1¼ cups **superfine sugar**
5 large **egg whites**
2 cups **unsalted butter** at room temperature
¾ cup **seedless strawberry jam**

For the simple vanilla syrup
¾ cup **superfine sugar**
2 tsp **vanilla extract**

For the decoration
1¼lb fresh **strawberries**

Materials
12in cardboard cake drum or cake stand
3 wooden or plastic dowel rods
6in thin cardboard cake round

As a kid I loved the idea of Neapolitan ice cream, but I was always disappointed with the taste. I always left the chocolate section, because so often the flavor just wasn't very nice. The color and flavors did, however, stay with me, and this modern wedding cake is inspired by that classic of the supermarket freezer aisle. Unlike traditional fruit or sponge wedding cakes, this cake is made with a genoise sponge as its base, and because of this it can actually be easily made in one day because it takes relatively little time to bake.

MY PARENTS' WEDDING DAY

1. To make the large vanilla cake, preheat the oven to 350°F, then grease and line a deep 9in cake pan with parchment paper, greasing the parchment too. Put the eggs, sugar, and vanilla in a large heatproof bowl set over a pan of gently simmering water, making sure the bottom of the bowl doesn't touch the water.

2. Whisk the eggs constantly until the sugar has dissolved and the mixture is just warm to the touch. Remove the bowl from the pan and, using an electric mixer, beat the eggs for 5 minutes on high speed, then reduce the speed to medium and beat for another 3 minutes. At this stage the mixture should form a very thick, slowly dissolving ribbon when the beaters are lifted from the bowl.

3. Sift the flour over the egg mixture and gently fold together, trying to keep as much volume as possible. Pour the cake batter into the prepared pan and lightly tap on the work surface to level out. Bake for 25–30 minutes, or until it springs back when lightly touched. Allow the cake to cool in the pan for 10 minutes before turning onto a wire rack to cool completely.

4. Repeat with the remaining mixtures using the appropriate pan sizes (9in for the large cakes and 6in for the small cakes). For the chocolate layers, whisk the cocoa powder and flour together, then sift the mixture over the egg mixture. Bake the 9in cakes for 25–30 minutes and the 6in cakes for 15–20 minutes, or until a skewer inserted into the middle of the cake comes out clean.

5. To make the buttercream, put ½ cup water and the sugar in a pan over medium heat, and have a sugar thermometer ready. Put the egg whites in a clean, grease-free bowl (this is best done using a freestanding electric mixer). As the syrup reaches about 240°F, start beating the eggs on high speed.

6. Cook until the syrup registers 250°F, then remove from the heat and, with the mixer still running, pour the syrup in a slow stream down the side of the bowl containing the whites, avoiding the beaters. Continue beating on high speed until the meringue is at room temperature.

7. With the mixer on medium-high, add the butter, a few pieces at a time, beating until fully combined. When adding the butter it can sometimes look curdled; if this happens, don't worry, just keep mixing and eventually it will smooth out again forming a light buttercream. Add the jam and mix to combine.

8. To make the simple syrup, put the sugar, vanilla, and ½ cup water in a small pan over high heat. Bring to a boil, then reduce the temperature and simmer for a few minutes until reduced slightly. Take the pan off the heat and set aside until needed.

9. To assemble the cake, use a serrated knife to cut each cake into three equal layers. Put a layer of either the large vanilla or chocolate cake onto the large cardboard cake drum or cake stand and brush with a layer of syrup. Top with a thin layer of the buttercream, spreading it so that it just peeks over the edge. Repeat the process, alternating the colors of the layers until all the larger cake layers are used.

10. Push the dowel rods into the cake about 3½in from the outer edge, in a triangle shape. Mark where the rods are level with the cake and then remove and cut them so that they sit flush with the top. Put the 6in cardboard cake round onto the large cake, sitting it on the dowels. Repeat the layering process with the 6in cakes and finish the cake by arranging the strawberries around the edges and on top of the cake.

TIP

It's an exceptionally light cake, but it is not intended to be stored. Make the cake as close to the wedding as possible, and no earlier than two days beforehand.

Macaron Tower

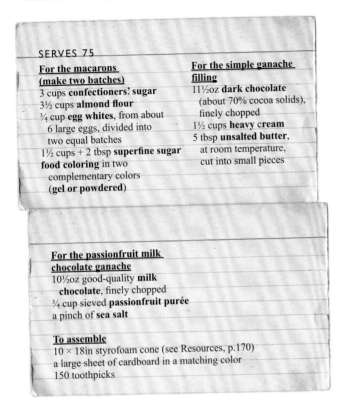

SERVES 75

**For the macarons
(make two batches)**
3 cups **confectioners' sugar**
3½ cups **almond flour**
¾ cup **egg whites**, from about
   6 large eggs, divided into
   two equal batches
1½ cups + 2 tbsp **superfine sugar**
food coloring in two
   complementary colors
   (gel or powdered)

**For the simple ganache
filling**
11½oz **dark chocolate**
   (about 70% cocoa solids),
   finely chopped
1½ cups **heavy cream**
5 tbsp **unsalted butter**,
   at room temperature,
   cut into small pieces

**For the passionfruit milk
chocolate ganache**
10½oz good-quality **milk
   chocolate**, finely chopped
¾ cup sieved **passionfruit purée**
a pinch of **sea salt**

To assemble
10 × 18in styrofoam cone (see Resources, p.170)
a large sheet of cardboard in a matching color
150 toothpicks

A macaron tower is about a million miles away from a traditional white wedding cake. You can be totally creative with the colors and flavors, and by making it yourself it will be significantly cheaper than buying a wedding cake. This recipe will take time, but you can make the batches of macarons over a week and then assemble them on the day. The effort will be worth it, because it will look spectacular. I have provided a simple dark chocolate ganache recipe for the filling as well as a passionfruit milk chocolate ganache, but you can use any flavored ganache if you prefer. Be creative—make the tower the way you want it to be for your special day.

1. You need to make two batches of macarons using the quantities given above for each batch, each using a different food coloring. Each batch requires five or six baking sheets. If you don't have that many, you can halve the recipe and make four batches instead (two in each of the colors).

2. Line five or six baking sheets with parchment paper. Put the confectioners' sugar and almond flour in the bowl of a food processor and pulse about 15 times until fully combined. Sift this mixture into a large bowl, discarding any small particles that remain.

3. Add the first batch of egg whites to the almond mixture and mix together to form a thick paste. Set aside.

4. Put ⅓ cup water and the superfine sugar into a small pan over medium heat. Bring to a boil and have a sugar thermometer ready. Meanwhile, put the remaining egg whites into a clean, grease-free bowl (this is best done using a freestanding electric mixer). Start beating the whites on high speed when the syrup in the pan reaches about 230°F on the sugar thermometer. Cook until the syrup registers 245°F. With the mixer still running, pour the syrup in a slow stream down the side of the bowl containing the whites, avoiding the beaters.

5. Continue to beat the meringue on high speed until the mixture has cooled and the bowl is no longer hot to the touch but is still a little warm. Add the food coloring and mix to combine.

6. Scrape the meringue onto the almond mixture and gently fold together. It is important at this stage not to over-mix the batter. The batter should fall in a thick ribbon from the spatula, fading back into the batter within about 30 seconds. If it doesn't, fold a few more times.

7. Add half the batter to a piping bag fitted with a large round piping tip. Pipe rounds about 1in in diameter onto the prepared baking sheets, repeating with the remaining batter. Let rest for 30 minutes or until the macarons have developed a skin and are no longer sticky. Preheat the oven to 325°F.

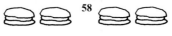

8. Bake the macarons for 12 minutes, then immediately slide the parchment paper onto the work surface and let cool for a few minutes before gently peeling the macarons off the paper. Let cool completely. Repeat steps 2–8 to make second batch of macarons.

9. To make the simple ganache, put the chocolate in a medium heatproof bowl and set aside. Put the cream in a small pan over medium heat and bring just to a boil. Pour in the chocolate and let stand for a few minutes before stirring gently to form a silky smooth ganache.

10. Add the butter and gently stir until just smooth and combined. Allow the filling to stand until thickened enough to pipe.

11. For the passionfruit milk chocolate ganache, put the chocolate in a medium heatproof bowl and set aside. Put the passionfruit purée and the salt in a medium pan, then place over medium heat and bring to a boil. Pour in the chocolate and let stand for a few minutes before stirring gently to combine. Let stand until thick enough to pipe; this ganache will take longer to thicken than the simple ganache.

12. Fill a piping bag fitted with a small plain piping tip with one of the ganaches and pipe onto half the macaron shells of one color. Sandwich with another macaron shell of the same color. Repeat with the other ganache and the other shells. (In the tower pictured I filled the purple with the simple ganache and the yellow with the passionfruit.) You can prepare the macarons ahead, if you like: freeze for up to one month or chill for up to five days.

13. To assemble the tower, wrap the styrofoam cone neatly with the cardboard (this is so that when the macarons are removed there won't be any styrofoam showing). To stick the macarons to the tower, push a toothpick through the paper into the styrofoam at a 45-degree angle leaving about ½in protruding. As you get nearer the top of the tower you will need to cut the toothpicks in half so that they don't poke out of the other side. Gently press the macaron onto the toothpick, making sure it doesn't poke through the front of the macaron. (The recipe should give you a few macarons extra in case any break or don't turn out successfully.)

14. To make the swirl pattern, use alternate colors of macarons, and when you start a new row put the macarons between the ones on the row below. Because it is unlikely that all your macarons will be perfectly the same size, decide which part of the cone you would like to be at the front, and then finish each row on the opposite side of the cone. This way any imperfections will be hidden on the back.

TIP

If making this for a
wedding, assemble the cake
on site as it is delicate
and is best not moved
once prepared.

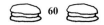

Wedding Cheesecake

SERVES 40

For the large (9in) cheesecake	For the small (6in) cheesecake
8oz **graham crackers**	3½oz **graham crackers**
½ cup **unsalted butter**, melted	3 tbsp **unsalted butter**, melted
4 cups (2lb) **full-fat cream cheese**	2 cups (1lb) **full-fat cream cheese**
2¼ cups **superfine sugar**	2 tbsp **superfine sugar**
1 tbsp **all-purpose flour**	1 tbsp **all-purpose flour**
4 large **eggs**, lightly beaten	2 large **eggs**, lightly beaten
1 tsp **vanilla bean paste**	1 tsp **vanilla bean paste**

To finish
9in and 6in cardboard cake rounds
4 plastic or wooden dowel rods
fresh flowers or fruit
ribbon (optional)

This is a small wedding cake that is perfect for a couple who wants something a little different. Many people don't like traditional wedding cakes, so it seems wasteful to spend hundreds of dollars on something that looks lovely but that people won't enjoy eating. This cake is ridiculously cheap in comparison to something more traditional, so it's also great for those watching the budget. Although this two-tiered cake is simple to achieve, you could, of course, increase the number of tiers; my boyfriend's sister has asked me to make her a 12-tiered cheesecake for her wedding—wish me luck!

1. For the large cheesecake, preheat the oven to 350°F and line the bottom of a 9in springform cake pan with parchment paper. Put the graham crackers in a medium bowl and, using the base of rolling pin, crush them into fine crumbs. Add the melted butter and stir to coat evenly.

2. Firmly press the mixture into the bottom and a little up the sides of the prepared pan. Bake for 10 minutes, then remove from the oven and let cool while you make the filling. Reduce the oven temperature to 300°F.

3. In the bowl of a freestanding electric mixer fitted with the paddle attachment, or using a hand-held electric mixer, beat the cream cheese until smooth and creamy, about 3 minutes. Add the sugar and flour and beat until combined—the less you beat a baked cheesecake mixture the better; if you over-beat, the cake will have a higher chance of developing cracks.

4. Beat in the eggs and vanilla paste, a little at a time, beating until just fully combined. Pour onto the graham cracker base and level out with a spatula. Bake for 1½ hours or until the edges are set but the center is still wobbly. Cool completely before chilling for 8 hours or until ready to serve.

5. Repeat to make the small cheesecake using a 6in springform cake pan and baking it for about 1 hour.

6. Once the cakes are thoroughly chilled you can assemble the cake. Put the large cake onto a 9in cardboard cake round and press 4 dowel rods in a square formation about 2½in from the outer edge, then mark where they are flush with the top of the cake. Now remove the dowels and cut them to fit, then push them back inside the cake. Put the small cake onto a 6in cardboard cake round and put this in the center of the larger cake, resting it on the dowels.

7. To decorate, put fresh flowers or fruit around the middle and on the top. If you want to make the cake look a little more traditional, you can also wrap the sides of the cakes with a piece of ribbon. Because the edge of the cake is moist, you will need to use a few layers of ribbon to make sure that no moisture bleeds through.

61

Wedding Cake Cookies

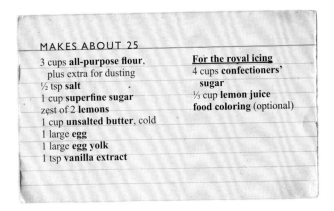

MAKES ABOUT 25

3 cups **all-purpose flour**,
plus extra for dusting
½ tsp **salt**
1 cup **superfine sugar**
zest of 2 **lemons**
1 cup **unsalted butter**, cold
1 large **egg**
1 large **egg yolk**
1 tsp **vanilla extract**

For the royal icing
4 cups **confectioners' sugar**
⅓ cup **lemon juice**
food coloring (optional)

These cookies are very cute and would make a really personal favor for any wedding. Although I have made the icing white, you could color the icing with a few drops of food coloring, and this way you can match the decoration of the cookies to the theme or style of the wedding. See page 168 for the template.

1. Line two baking sheets with parchment paper. Put the flour, salt, sugar, and lemon zest in the bowl of a food processor and pulse to combine. Add the butter and pulse until the mixture resembles coarse bread crumbs. (Alternatively, mix the dry ingredients in a large bowl and rub the butter into the flour by hand or using a pastry cutter.) Add the egg, yolk, and vanilla extract and pulse, or stir, until the mixture just comes together. Transfer to a lightly floured work surface and gently knead together until uniform. Divide the dough in half and wrap in plastic wrap, then chill for about 1 hour.

2. Remove the dough from the fridge and let rest for 10 minutes before rolling out. Working with one half of the dough at a time, roll out to a thickness of ¼in. Using a wedding cake-shaped cookie cutter or template (see page 168), cut out as many cookies as possible. Re-roll the scraps to cut out more cookies. Lift the cookies off the surface with a metal spatula and put onto the baking sheet. Chill for 15–20 minutes. Meanwhile, preheat the oven to 350°F.

3. Bake the cookies for 15–18 minutes or until the edges turn golden. Let cool on the baking sheets for 10 minutes before transferring to a wire rack to cool completely.

4. To make the royal icing, put the confectioners' sugar in a large bowl and add the lemon juice. Using a wooden spoon, mix gently to incorporate the two together. Once combined, beat the mixture until you have a thick and smooth paste. If you want to color the icing, add a few drops of your chosen color.

5. To decorate the cookies, put the icing into a piping bag fitted with a thin plain piping tube, about ⅛in wide. Pipe the icing around the outline of the cookies and then pipe on your decorations. You can pipe whatever decoration comes to mind; one of the simplest is a crosshatch pattern. Once decorated, allow the icing to dry for a few hours.

TIP

If you would like your cookies to have a bit of glam, sprinkle some edible glitter or colored sugar onto the icing while it is still wet to add a bit of sparkle.

Salted Caramel Truffles

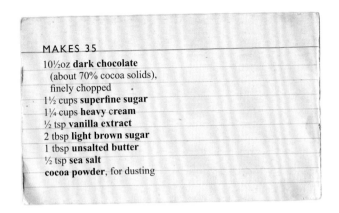

MAKES 35

10½oz **dark chocolate**
(about 70% cocoa solids),
finely chopped
1½ cups **superfine sugar**
1¼ cups **heavy cream**
½ tsp **vanilla extract**
2 tbsp **light brown sugar**
1 tbsp **unsalted butter**
½ tsp **sea salt**
cocoa powder, for dusting

The flavors of salted caramel and chocolate make a delicious combination. These truffles are super-easy to prepare and would make perfect favors for a wedding—and homemade is always so much more special than bought.

1. Put the chocolate in a medium heatproof bowl and set aside. Put the superfine sugar in a medium pan over medium heat and leave until the sugar begins to dissolve and caramelize around the edges. Using a silicon spatula, drag the dissolved sugar toward the middle to help it dissolve evenly.

2. Once the sugar is fully dissolved and has turned a dark golden brown color, pour in half the cream and all the vanilla and light brown sugar; it will bubble up furiously, so be careful and go slowly. Once the bubbling has subsided, add the remaining cream. If the caramel is lumpy, put over low heat and allow to melt. Once you have a smooth caramel, add the butter and sea salt and stir gently to combine.

3. Pour the hot caramel over the chocolate and gently stir to combine. Chill for a couple of hours until firm enough to form into balls.

4. To make the truffles, have a small bowl of cocoa powder ready and a baking sheet lined with parchment paper. Take large teaspoons of the ganache mixture and roll into balls, then roll in the cocoa powder and set on the baking sheet. Chill the truffles until needed.

TIP

If the ganache splits when you add the caramel, use a hand blender to bring it back together.

Mexican Wedding Cookies

MAKES 40

1 cup **unsalted butter**	**For the coating**
¾ cup **confectioners' sugar**	1 cup **confectioners' sugar**
1 tsp **vanilla extract** .	1 tsp **ground cinnamon**
2 cups **all-purpose flour**, plus extra for dusting	
1 cup **pecans**, finely chopped	
1 tsp **ground cinnamon**	
½ tsp **sea salt**	

These cookies go by many different names, including Russian tea cakes and butterballs. Normally they are made in the same way as most cookies and are domed and look like snowballs (which is another name for them), but as wedding favors I think they look a little more elegant rolled and cut into rounds. The cookies are covered in confectioners' sugar and cinnamon after baking.

1. Line two baking sheets with parchment paper. Put the butter, confectioners' sugar, and vanilla into the bowl of a food processor and pulse until smooth and creamy. Add the flour, pecans, cinnamon, and salt and pulse until evenly combined. (Alternatively, beat together the butter, confectioners' sugar, and vanilla, then stir in the flour, pecans, cinnamon, and salt until fully combined.) Transfer the dough onto a lightly floured work surface and form into a circle. Wrap with plastic wrap and chill for 30 minutes.

2. Dust the work surface with a little flour and roll out the dough until it is about ¼in thick. Cut out circles using a 2in cookie cutter. Place on the prepared baking sheet and chill for 15 minutes or until firm. Preheat the oven to 350°F.

3. Bake the cookies for 12–14 minutes or until the edges are golden brown. Let cool on the pan for 10 minutes before transferring to a wire rack to cool.

4. Meanwhile, make the coating. Mix the confectioners' sugar and cinnamon together in a small bowl. When the cookies are no longer hot but still slightly warm, coat them in the confectioners' sugar mixture. Stored in a sealed container, these cookies will keep well for about four days.

Apple Strudel

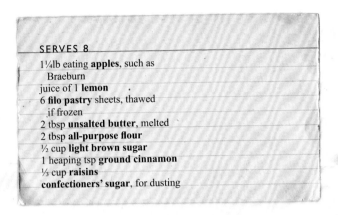

SERVES 8

1¼lb eating **apples**, such as
  Braeburn
juice of 1 **lemon**
6 **filo pastry** sheets, thawed
  if frozen
2 tbsp **unsalted butter**, melted
2 tbsp **all-purpose flour**
½ cup **light brown sugar**
1 heaping tsp **ground cinnamon**
⅓ cup **raisins**
confectioners' sugar, for dusting

Apple strudel is one of those dishes that I hadn't eaten for years until recently, although it was a firm favorite when I was little, and I seem to remember eating it at my friends' houses a lot when I was a kid. Technically, this isn't a genuine strudel, because it doesn't use strudel pastry but, frankly, as much as I love making pastry, strudel dough isn't the easiest to use; it has to be stretched wafer thin using your hands, and although it is delicious I am happy using store-bought filo pastry for a fast and tasty homemade version.

1. Preheat the oven to 375°F and line a baking sheet with parchment paper. Peel and core the apples, then slice them into thin wedges and put them into a large bowl with the lemon juice. This will keep the apples from browning.

2. Put a sheet of filo pastry on the prepared baking sheet and brush lightly with the melted butter (cover the unused pastry with a damp kitchen towel). Cover with a second sheet of filo and repeat the process until all six sheets have been used.

3. Drain the lemon juice from the apples and toss with the all-purpose flour, sugar, cinnamon, and raisins. Put the apple mixture along the long edge of the pastry and roll up to form the strudel, squeezing the ends together to seal. Bake for 30–40 minutes or until the pastry is crisp and golden. Let cool slightly, then dust with a little confectioners' sugar before serving.

67

Springtime Blossom Cake

SERVES 12

1 cup + ¾ stick **unsalted butter**, at room temp, plus extra	4⅔ cups **confectioners' sugar**
1½ cups **superfine sugar**	pinch of **salt**
5 large **eggs**, lightly beaten	**To finish**
2 tsp **vanilla extract**	¼ cup **raspberry jam**
2 cups **self-rising flour**	**confectioners' sugar**, for dusting
½ cup **sour cream**	1¼lb **white fondant**
For the vanilla buttercream	3½oz **peach fondant**
1 cup + 2 tbsp **unsalted butter**, at room temperature	3½oz **violet fondant**
⅓ cup **heavy cream**	a little **royal icing**
1 tsp **vanilla bean paste**	**nonpareils** (optional)

This cake is simple to put together, but the decoration does take a little time. It's perfect to show your loved one that you have put in a bit of effort! To help create level layers, make sure the cake is fully cooled, and then chill in the fridge for 10 minutes, as this will lead to fewer crumbs when slicing the cake into halves. Make sure all the cake ingredients are at room temperature, so they will blend together more easily and create a lighter cake.

1. Preheat the oven to 350°F, then grease and line a deep 9in cake pan with parchment paper, greasing the parchment too. Put the butter in a large bowl and, using an electric mixer, beat until smooth and creamy, about 3 minutes. Add the sugar and beat until light and fluffy, about 5 minutes.

2. Add the eggs, a little at a time, beating well after each addition and scraping down the bowl when needed. Once the eggs are fully incorporated, add the vanilla extract and half the flour, and beat until just combined. Add the sour cream and mix to combine, then add the remaining flour and beat until fully combined, but be careful not to over-mix.

3. Pour the batter into the prepared pan and bake for 1 hour 20 minutes or until the cake springs back when lightly touched or a skewer inserted into the center comes out clean. Allow the cake to cool in the pan for 20 minutes before turning onto a wire rack to cool completely.

4. To make the buttercream, put the butter in a large bowl and, using an electric mixer, beat until light and creamy, about 3 minutes. Slowly pour in the cream and add the vanilla paste, mixing until fully combined. Add the confectioners' sugar and salt, a little at a time, beating until fully combined. Once the sugar is fully incorporated, turn the mixer to high and beat until the buttercream is light and fluffy.

5. To assemble the cake, put the cake onto a cardboard cake board or serving plate. If the cake is domed, use a serrated knife to level it, then slice the cake in half. Spread jam on the base cake. Spread a thick layer of buttercream on the bottom of the top half of cake. Sandwich the layers together, then cover the top and sides of the cake with a smooth layer of buttercream.

6. To decorate, dust a clean work surface with a small amount of confectioners' sugar and knead the white fondant until pliable. Roll the fondant until it is large enough to cover the cake. The easiest way to do this is to take a piece of string and use it as a guide. Drape it over the cake and grip it where it meets the table. Lift the string from the cake and use this as a measure for your fondant. Using the flats of your hands and arms, drape the fondant over the cake and use the palms of your hands to smooth the top, applying gentle pressure. Carefully work your way around the cake, gently smoothing the fondant onto the sides, trimming off the excess.

7. To create the decorations, roll the peach and violet fondants until thin and, using different-sized blossom cutters, press out as many flowers as you can. To give the flowers some body, put each into your palm and gently press in the center of the flower. This keeps them from being completely flat and gives the cake more visual appeal.

8. If you want to go a step further, you can add a white nonpareil to the center of each, gently pressing it into the fondant. Allow the flowers to dry out for 2 hours before attaching them to the cake. To stick the flowers to the cake, pipe a small amount of royal icing to the back of the flowers and gently stick them to the cake.

Orange & Chocolate 50th Anniversary Cake

SERVES 12

1 cup **unsalted butter**
   at room temperature,
   plus extra for greasing
2¼ cups **all-purpose flour**
⅓ cup **cornstarch**
4½ tsp **baking powder**
½ tsp **salt**
1¾ cups **superfine sugar**
zest of 2 large **oranges**
1 tsp **vanilla extract**
4 medium **eggs**

1¼ cups **buttermilk**
edible gold powder,
   to decorate

For the orange Italian meringue buttercream
1¼ cups **superfine sugar**
6 medium **egg whites**
2 cups **unsalted butter** at
   room temperature
1½ cups **orange curd**, available
   at gourmet supermarkets

For the chocolate glaze
5½oz **dark chocolate**
   (about 70% cocoa solids)
¾ cup heavy cream

I have very strong memories of my grandparents' 50th anniversary. The whole family got together and we had a party. For presents, we bought 50 gifts, some silly little things but each and every one was related to gold, the traditional gift for a 50th anniversary. There was everything from a gold photo frame to gold-wrapped chocolates. If only we had served this golden cake, everything would have been tinged with gold.

1. Preheat the oven to 350°F, then grease and line three 8in cake pans with parchment paper, greasing the parchment too. In a medium bowl whisk the flour, cornstarch, baking powder, and salt together to combine, then set aside.

2. Put the butter in a large bowl. Using an electric mixer, beat the butter on medium-high speed until smooth and light, add the sugar and orange zest, and beat until light and fluffy, about 5 minutes. Add the vanilla and mix to combine. With the mixer on medium speed, beat in the eggs, a little at a time, beating until fully combined before adding the next. With the mixer on low, add the flour mixture in three additions, alternating with the buttermilk, starting and finishing with the flour. Divide the batter between the prepared pans and bake for 25–30 minutes or until the cakes are golden brown and spring back when lightly touched. Let cool in the pans for 10 minutes before turning onto wire racks to cool completely.

3. To make the meringue buttercream, put ¼ cup water and the sugar in a pan over medium heat. Bring to a boil and have a sugar thermometer ready. Meanwhile, put the egg whites into a clean, grease-free bowl (this is best done using a freestanding electric mixer). Start beating the whites on high speed when the syrup in the pan reaches about 240°F on the sugar thermometer. Cook until the syrup registers 250°F. With the mixer still running, pour the syrup in a slow stream down the side of the bowl containing the whites, avoiding the beaters. Continue beating on high speed until the meringue is at room temperature.

4. With the mixer on medium-high speed, add the butter, a few pieces at a time, beating until fully combined. When adding the butter it can sometimes look curdled; don't worry, just keep mixing and eventually it will smooth out to form a light buttercream. Add 1 cup of the orange curd and mix until fully combined.

5. To assemble the cake, put the first cake layer onto a cardboard cake round, cake stand, or serving plate and top with a layer of buttercream. Add half the remaining orange curd and repeat the process with the second layer of cake, finishing with the final layer of cake. Use the remaining buttercream to coat the top and sides. Using a long offset spatula, smooth the buttercream so that the tops and sides are perfectly smooth. Put the cake in the fridge for 15 minutes while you make the glaze.

6. Put the chocolate in a medium heatproof bowl and set aside. Put the cream in a small pan over medium heat. When the cream comes to a boil, remove from the heat and pour in the chocolate. Let stand for a couple of minutes before stirring together to form a silky smooth ganache. Pour the ganache over the chilled cake, teasing it over the edges so that it drips down the buttercream. Before the ganache fully sets, dip a small paintbrush into edible gold powder and flick the powder over the chocolate to give the cake a golden shimmer.

festive

S'mores Cake

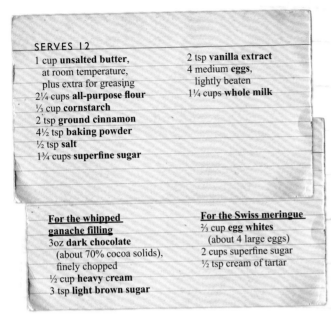

SERVES 12

1 cup **unsalted butter**,
  at room temperature,
  plus extra for greasing
2¼ cups **all-purpose flour**
⅓ cup **cornstarch**
2 tsp **ground cinnamon**
4½ tsp **baking powder**
½ tsp **salt**
1¾ cups **superfine sugar**

2 tsp **vanilla extract**
4 medium **eggs**,
  lightly beaten
1¼ cups **whole milk**

For the whipped ganache filling
3oz **dark chocolate**
  (about 70% cocoa solids),
  finely chopped
½ cup **heavy cream**
3 tsp **light brown sugar**

For the Swiss meringue
⅔ cup **egg whites**
  (about 4 large eggs)
2 cups superfine sugar
½ tsp cream of tartar

When I was a child I was a boy scout, and although it wasn't really my thing, one of the few activities that I really did enjoy was the campfires and roasted marshmallows served between graham crackers. This simple treat is perfectly delicious as it is, but it was taken a step further when someone decided to add chocolate—and everything is better with chocolate! As the name suggests, you will always want s'more!

1. Preheat the oven to 350°F, then grease and line three 8in round cake pans with parchment paper, greasing the parchment too. In a medium bowl whisk the flour, cornstarch, cinnamon, baking powder, and salt together to combine, then set aside.

2. Put the butter in a large bowl. Using an electric mixer, beat the butter on medium-high speed until smooth and light, add the sugar, and beat until light and fluffy, about 5 minutes. Add the vanilla and mix to combine. With the mixer on medium speed, add the eggs, a little at a time, beating until fully combined before adding more. With the mixer on low, add the flour mixture in three additions, alternating with the milk, starting and finishing with the flour.

3. Divide the batter evenly among the prepared pans and bake for 30–35 minutes or until the cake is golden brown and springs back when lightly touched. Let the cakes cool in the pans for 10 minutes before turning onto a wire rack to cool completely.

4. To make the ganache filling, put the chocolate in a medium heatproof bowl. Put the cream and sugar in a small pan over medium heat and bring just to a boil. Immediately, pour the hot cream over the chocolate and let stand for a few minutes before gently stirring together to form a smooth silky ganache. Chill the ganache until cool and slightly thickened, but not set. Using a whisk, beat until thickened. Spread the ganache across two of the cake layers and set aside while you make the Swiss meringue.

5. Put the egg whites, sugar, and cream of tartar in a heatproof bowl set over a pan of gently simmering water, and whisk constantly until the sugar has dissolved and the egg whites are warm to the touch. Remove the bowl from the heat and, using an electric mixer, beat until the meringue forms stiff glossy peaks. (When you have made the meringue, you need to work with it fairly quickly. Don't let it stand or it will firm up too much to spread easily.)

6. To assemble the cake, put the first cake layer topped with chocolate onto a cake stand or serving plate and spread with a thin layer of the meringue. Repeat with the second chocolate-topped cake layer and finish with the final layer. Take the remaining meringue and spread across the top and sides of the cake—this doesn't have to look perfect, as any imperfections will just add to the effect. To finish the cake, take a blowtorch and lightly torch the meringue until it is golden.

Pecan Pie Cake

SERVES 10

1 cup **unsalted butter** at room
   temperature, plus extra
   for greasing
2 cups **pecans**
1 cup **almond flour**
1 cup **light brown sugar**
2 tbsp **maple syrup**
4 large **eggs**, lightly beaten
½ cup **all-purpose flour**
1 tsp **baking powder**
¼ tsp **salt**
¼ cup **maple syrup**

I love pecan pie. It is one of those seasonal dishes that I could happily eat all year round. Sometimes I want something a little less sugary and easier to make than the pie, and this cake is just that recipe—perfect for a lazy weekend treat. The simple cake is made with almond flour and pecans with the warm flavor of maple syrup.

1. Preheat the oven to 350°F. Lightly grease and line a deep 8in cake pan with parchment paper, greasing the parchment too. Put the pecans on a baking sheet and put in the oven to toast for 5 minutes or until fragrant. Watch the nuts carefully, as they burn easily.

2. Put half the pecans and all the almond flour into the bowl of a food processor and pulse until they are fairly fine. You won't get the pecans as fine as the almonds but that doesn't matter.

3. Put the butter in a large bowl and, using an electric mixer, beat until light and creamy, about 3 minutes. Add the light brown sugar and maple syrup and beat until light and fluffy, about 5 minutes. Add the eggs, a little a time, beating until fully combined. Sift the flour, baking powder, and salt into the bowl with the nuts and mix to combine evenly. Add this mixture to the butter mixture and fold to combine. Pour the batter into the prepared pan and gently level out.

4. Bake for 50–55 minutes or until the cake is golden brown and springs backs when lightly touched. If the cake browns too quickly, put a tent of foil over the top.

5. While the cake is baking, make the topping by roughly chopping the remaining pecans and mixing them with the maple syrup. Remove the cake from the oven and cool in the pan for 10 minutes before turning onto a wire rack. Sprinkle the topping over the cake and let cool before serving.

76

Salted Caramel Apple Pie

SERVES 8

3½ cups **all-purpose flour**, plus extra for dusting	2 tsp **unsalted butter** a large pinch of **sea salt**
1 tsp **salt**	**For the apple filling**
2 tbsp **superfine sugar**	2¾lb **apples**, such as a mixture of Granny Smith and Braeburn
1 cup + 1 tbsp **unsalted butter**, chilled and diced	
½–⅔ cup ice-cold **water**	1 tsp **lemon juice**
1 large **egg** mixed with 1 tbsp **water**	1½ tsp **cinnamon**
	½ tsp freshly grated **nutmeg**
For the salted caramel filling	3 tbsp **cornstarch**
¾ cup **superfine sugar**	
⅓ cup **heavy cream**	

Apple pie is classic comfort food—and I love it—but when I heard about a bakery in New York that had added salted caramel, I knew I had to come up with my own version. The caramel recipe makes a little more than needed, but you can use it when serving the pie, along with a scoop of vanilla ice cream, of course.

1. To make the salted caramel filling, put the superfine sugar in a medium pan over medium heat and leave until the sugar begins to dissolve and caramelize around the edges. Using a silicon spatula, drag the dissolved sugar toward the middle to help it dissolve evenly.

2. Once the sugar is fully dissolved and has turned a dark golden brown color, pour in half the cream; it will bubble up furiously, so be careful and go slowly. Once the bubbling has subsided, add the remaining cream. If the caramel is lumpy, put over low heat and let melt. Once you have a smooth caramel, add the butter and sea salt, and stir gently to combine. Pour the caramel into a bowl to cool until needed.

3. Put the flour, salt, and sugar in the bowl of a food processor and pulse to combine. Add the chilled butter and pulse until it forms small chunks, just under the size of a pea. Slowly add the water while pulsing the food processor until the dough holds together when squeezed. (Alternatively, mix the dry ingredients in a bowl and add the butter. Rub together with your fingertips until the butter pieces are just under the size of a pea. Slowly stir in the water, using a fork, until the dough holds together.) If you add too much water the dough will become too soft. Transfer the dough to the work surface and gently knead together. Divide into two balls, one a little larger than the other. Wrap in plastic wrap and chill for 30 minutes.

4. Lightly dust the work surface with flour and roll out the larger piece of dough until it is large enough to line a 9in pie dish. Gently roll the dough around your rolling pin, and then drape over the pie dish. Press the dough into the dish and then trim the excess, leaving a 1in overhang. Take the second piece of dough and roll out as before, then put the pastry on a baking sheet. Chill the lined pie dish and the rolled dough while you make the filling.

5. Peel, core, and slice the apples, adding them to a large bowl with the lemon juice to prevent browning. Add the cinnamon, nutmeg, and cornstarch and toss together to coat evenly.

6. To assemble the pie, remove the dough from the fridge and place a third of the apples into the lined pie dish. Top with about a quarter of the caramel and then repeat the process with the remaining two-thirds of the apples. Brush the dough overhang with a little of the egg wash (the egg and water mixed together) and then drape the remaining dough on top of the pie.

7. Trim the excess, leaving you with a 1in overhang. Roll the excess dough under itself to form the pie's edge. To crimp the pie, pinch together the thumb and forefinger of one hand against the edge of the pie crust and, using the index finger of the other, press the dough together along the top edge to form a simple scallop. Chill the prepared pie for 30 minutes before baking. Preheat the oven to 400°F.

8. Brush the pie with egg wash and, using a sharp knife, cut a few vent holes in the top of the pastry. Bake for 10 minutes, then reduce the temperature to 375°F and bake for another 1 hour or until the dough is golden and the filling is bubbling. If the dough is browning too fast, put a tent of foil over the top. Let cool before serving.

Cherry Pie

SERVES 8

1 cup **superfine sugar**
1¾lb pitted or frozen **cherries**
zest and juice of 1 **lemon**
⅓ cup **cornstarch**

For the dough
3 cups **all-purpose flour**,
 plus extra for dusting
1 tsp **salt**
2 tbsp **superfine sugar**

1 cup + 6 tbsp **unsalted
 butter**, diced and chilled
about ⅓ cup ice-cold **water**
1 medium **egg**, beaten
 with 1 tbsp **water**

Cherry pie is one of those desserts that is quintessentially American. Because cherries can be quite watery, I make the filling in a pan. This helps to lower the risk of a watery filling, which would make the dough soggy. As the season for fresh cherries is fairly short, I normally make this with frozen cherries so that I can have the pie all year round.

1. Put the sugar, 1¼lb of the cherries, and the lemon zest in a large pan over medium heat. Put the cornstarch and lemon juice in a small bowl and mix to form a smooth paste. As the cherries begin to release their juice, add this paste to the pan and cook the cherries gently, stirring, until the juice comes to a boil. Cook, stirring, for a few more minutes until thickened. Remove from the heat and add the reserved cherries. Set aside to cool while you make the dough.

2. Put the flour, salt, and sugar in the bowl of a food processor and pulse to combine. Add the chilled butter and pulse until it forms small chunks, just under the size of a pea. Slowly add the water while pulsing the food processor until the dough holds together when squeezed. (Alternatively, mix the dry ingredients in a bowl and add the butter. Rub together with your fingertips until the butter pieces are just under the size of a pea. Slowly stir in the water, using a fork, until the dough holds together.) If you add too much water the dough will be too soft. Transfer the dough to the work surface and gently knead together. Divide into two balls, one a little larger than the other. Wrap in plastic wrap and chill for 30 minutes.

3. Lightly dust the work surface with flour and roll out the larger piece of dough, until it is large enough to line a 9in pie dish. Gently roll the dough around your rolling pin, and then drape it over the pie dish. Press the dough into the dish and then trim the excess, leaving a 1in overhang. Take the second piece of dough and roll out as before. Using a knife or pizza cutter, cut the dough into strips 1in thick. Put the pie dish and the strips of dough in the fridge for 15 minutes to let the dough rest.

4. Preheat the oven to 400°F. Remove the pie dish and strips of dough from the fridge and pour the filling into the prepared base. Brush the edge of the pie and the overhang with a little egg and water wash, and then lay half the dough strips over the pie. Brush the strips with egg, then put the second half of strips at a 90-degree angle from the first half creating a very simple lattice pattern. As before, brush the lattice with egg wash.

5. To finish the pie, fold the dough overhang so that it sits on the rim of the dish and covers the edges of the dough strips. To crimp the pie, pinch together the thumb and forefinger of one hand against the edge of the pie crust and, using the index finger of the other, press the dough together along the top edge to form a simple scallop. Bake for 40–45 minutes or until the dough is golden and the filling is bubbling.

Crêpe Cake

SERVES 8

1 cup plus 1 tbsp **all-purpose flour**	**For the filling**
2 tbsp **superfine sugar**	1 cup **heavy cream**
¼ tsp **salt**	½ cup **lemon curd,** available at gourmet supermarkets
2 large **eggs**	⅔ cup **raspberry jam**
⅔ cup **whole milk**	
2 tbsp **unsalted butter**, melted and cooled	
vegetable oil, for greasing	
confectioners' sugar, for dusting	

Sometimes you don't want a layered cake but something different and lighter. This crêpe cake is easy to prepare and would make a lovely Easter dessert. I have filled it with lemon and jam, but you could use other ingredients such as chocolate cream and pistachios, perhaps—whatever you feel like.

1. Put the flour, sugar, and salt in a large bowl and whisk together, then make a well in the center. In a medium bowl whisk together the eggs, milk, and ½ cup water, then pour this into the flour mixture and whisk together until smooth. Pour in the melted butter and whisk to combine. Cover the bowl with plastic wrap and chill for 1 hour before cooking.

2. To cook the crêpes, lightly grease an 8in frying pan with vegetable oil and heat the pan over medium-high heat. When the pan is hot, pour a small ladleful of the batter into the center of the pan and swirl gently to spread it evenly across the surface.

3. Cook until the crêpe begins to brown around the edge, then flip it over and cook for a few more minutes on the other side until lightly golden. When cooked, pile the crêpes onto a sheet of parchment paper to cool while you make the rest. Repeat with the remaining batter—you should have about 12 crêpes.

4. To make the filling, lightly whisk the heavy cream in a large bowl until it holds soft peaks. Add the lemon curd and whisk until combined and the cream is light and fluffy.

5. To assemble the cake, put the first crêpe onto a serving plate or cake stand and spread with a layer of the lemon cream. Top with a second crêpe and spread this with a thin layer of jam. Repeat this process, layering up the crêpes until you have a towering stack. You can serve immediately or, if you prefer a slightly firmer filling, chill for 1 hour. Before serving, dust with a little confectioners' sugar.

Chocolate Orange Hot Cross Buns

MAKES 8

2¾ cups **bread flour**,
  plus extra for dusting
½ tsp **salt**
2 tsp **pumpkin pie spice**
¼ cup **superfine sugar**
¼oz **instant yeast**
zest of 1 **orange**
1 large **egg**
¾ cup **whole milk**, lukewarm
2 tbsp **unsalted butter**,
  melted and cooled

½ cup **raisins**
2½oz **dark chocolate**
  (about 70% cocoa solids),
  roughly chopped
oil, for greasing

For the crosses
⅓ cup **bread flour**
2 tbsp **honey**, warmed

For me hot cross buns shout out "Easter!": the smell, the taste, and the nostalgia of them. And while I do love the classic, my little twist makes them even more delicious by adding some dark chocolate to the dough. If you prefer the classic and want to omit the chocolate, increase the raisins to ¾ cup and add 1 tsp ground cinnamon.

1. Line a baking sheet with parchment paper. Sift the flour, salt, mixed spice, and sugar into a large bowl and add the yeast and orange zest. In a small bowl mix the egg, milk, and melted butter together until combined, then pour into the flour mixture. Using a rounded knife or your hands, mix together to make a soft dough.

2. Lightly flour the work surface and transfer the dough onto it. Knead the dough for 5 minutes or until it is smooth and elastic. Flatten the dough, then sprinkle over the raisins and chocolate. Fold over the dough to seal the chocolate and raisins inside, then knead for 2 minutes to evenly distribute them. Form into a ball, put into a lightly oiled bowl, and cover with plastic wrap. Put in a warm place and let rise for 1 hour or until doubled in size.

3. Transfer the dough to the floured work surface and lightly knead to knock out some of the air. Divide the dough into eight equal pieces and form into balls. Put the balls onto the baking sheet about 2in apart. Lightly cover with plastic wrap and let rise for 40 minutes, or until doubled in size. Meanwhile, preheat the oven to 425°F.

4. To make the cross, put the flour and ¼ cup water in a bowl and mix to form a thick paste. Spoon the paste into a piping bag and pipe crosses on the buns. Bake for 20–25 minutes or until risen and golden. While still warm, brush the buns with the warmed honey.

Easter Nest Cupcakes

MAKES 12

1½ cups **all-purpose flour**	1 cup + 1 tbsp **unsalted**
2 tsp **baking powder**	**butter** at room temperature
¼ tsp **salt**	1 tbsp **heavy cream**
1 cup **unsalted butter** at	1½ cups **confectioners'**
room temperature	**sugar**
1 cup + 2 tbsp **superfine sugar**	pinch of **salt**
4 large **eggs**, lightly beaten	**For the decoration**
½ cup **whole milk**	3½oz **dark chocolate**
For the chocolate frosting	(about 70% cocoa solids)
4oz **dark chocolate**	in one piece
(about 70% cocoa solids),	36 **mini chocolate eggs**
finely chopped	

At Easter I always remember there being little Easter egg nests made of cornflakes coated in chocolate and then topped with some mini eggs. These cupcakes are a different spin on that same idea, and a perfect activity to keep kids occupied over the Easter holiday.

1. Preheat the oven to 350°F and line a standard 12-cup muffin pan with paper liners. In a medium bowl whisk the flour, baking powder, and salt together to combine, then set aside.

2. Put the butter in a large bowl and, using an electric mixer, beat on high speed until light and creamy, about 3 minutes. Add the sugar and beat on high speed until light and fluffy, about 5 minutes.

3. Beat in the eggs, a little at a time, beating until fully combined, then add the flour mixture in three additions, alternating with the milk, starting and finishing with the flour. Divide the batter among the prepared muffin cups, and bake for 20–25 minutes or until a toothpick inserted into the center of a cake comes out clean. Allow the cakes to cool in the pan for 10 minutes before transferring to a wire rack to cool completely.

4. To make the frosting, melt the chocolate in a heatproof bowl set over a pan of gently simmering water, making sure the bottom of the bowl doesn't touch the water. Remove from the heat and let cool slightly. Put the butter in a large bowl and, using an electric mixer, beat until light and smooth, about 3 minutes. Slowly incorporate the cream, then slowly add the confectioners' sugar and salt, and beat until light and creamy. Pour in the melted chocolate and mix to combine. If the frosting is too liquid, chill for 10 minutes or until slightly thickened.

5. To decorate, spread the frosting across the tops of the cooled cupcakes and then, using a sharp knife or a vegetable peeler, grate the bar of chocolate to create shards. Scatter these over the cupcakes. Top each cake with three mini eggs to finish.

84

Simnel Cake

SERVES 12

¾ cup **golden raisins**	1 tsp **pumpkin pie spice**
¾ cup **raisins**	¾ cup **unsalted butter**,
¾ cup **currants**	at room temperature
2½oz **mixed candied peel**	¾ cup + 2 tbsp **superfine sugar**
zest of 1 **lemon**	3 large **eggs**, lightly beaten
zest of 1 **orange**	**confectioners' sugar**,
3 tbsp **brandy**	for dusting
1¼ cups **all-purpose flour**	1lb **marzipan**
1 cup **almond flour**	a little **apricot jam**,
¼ tsp **salt**	melted and sieved
1 tsp **ground cinnamon**	1 **egg**, lightly beaten

A simnel cake is pure Easter: the meaning of the cake is based around the 12 disciples, and the 11 marzipan balls represent the "true disciples"—Judas having been omitted. Whatever the history of the cake, it is a delicious fruit cake with a layer of marzipan baked into the center—the perfect match!

1. The night before you want to make the cake, put the fruits, zests, and brandy in a large bowl and mix together. Cover with plastic wrap and let soak overnight.

2. The next day, preheat the oven to 300°F, then grease and triple-line a deep 8in cake pan with parchment paper. In a medium bowl whisk the all-purpose and almond flours, salt, and spices together to combine, then set aside.

3. Put the butter and sugar in a large bowl and, using an electric mixer, beat until light and fluffy, about 5 minutes. Beat in the eggs, a little at a time, mixing until fully combined. With the mixer on low, add the flour mixture, a large spoonful at a time, mixing until just combined. Using a large spatula or metal spoon, fold in the fruit.

4. Dust the work surface with confectioners' sugar and roll out a third of the marzipan, then cut it into an 8in circle. Scrape half the batter into the prepared cake pan and level out. Put the circle of marzipan onto the cake and top with the remaining cake batter. Bake for 1¾ hours or until a toothpick inserted into the center comes out clean. If the cake is browning too fast, make a tent with foil and put it over the top. Let the cake cool completely in the pan before removing.

5. To finish the cake, brush the top with a little melted apricot jam. Roll out half the remaining marzipan and cut out another 8in circle. Put this on the top of the cake. Divide the remaining marzipan into 11 equal pieces and roll into balls. Using a little apricot jam as glue, stick the balls around the edge of the cake.

6. Brush the marzipan balls and disc with a little beaten egg and then, using a blowtorch, lightly brown the marzipan, or put the cake under a hot broiler for 1–2 minutes.

Macadamia & Cranberry Cake

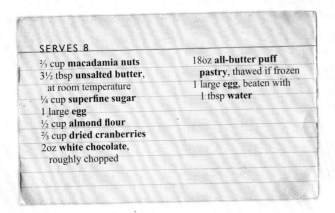

SERVES 8

⅔ cup **macadamia nuts**
3½ tbsp **unsalted butter**,
  at room temperature
¼ cup **superfine sugar**
1 large **egg**
½ cup **almond flour**
⅔ cup **dried cranberries**
2oz **white chocolate**,
  roughly chopped

18oz **all-butter puff**
  pastry, thawed if frozen
1 large **egg**, beaten with
  1 tbsp **water**

This isn't really a cake, it's a version of a French dish called "king's cake," which is basically an almond frangipane sandwiched between layers of puff pastry. While it can be made for any occasion, I prefer it for New Year's Day. My take on this classic is a filling made with rich macadamia nuts as well as almonds, with the addition of white chocolate and cranberries. The result is creamy with hits of fruits—a lovely dish that's very easy to make.

1. Line a baking sheet with parchment paper. Grind ⅓ of the macadamia nuts in a food processor; be careful not to over-process them, as they will turn into nut butter if you try to grind them as finely as almond flour. Roughly chop the remaining macadamia nuts and set aside.

2. To make the frangipane, beat the butter and sugar together until light and fluffy. Beat in the egg, a little at a time, followed by the almonds and both the ground and chopped macadamia nuts. Add the cranberries and the chocolate, and mix to combine.

3. Roll out the pastry to ⅛in thick and cut out two circles 10½in in diameter. Put one circle on the prepared baking sheet and the other on a sheet of parchment paper and chill for 30 minutes. Preheat the oven to 350°F.

4. Spread the frangipane in an even layer over the pastry round on the baking sheet, leaving a 1in border. Brush the pastry border with the egg wash. Lay the second disc of pastry on top and gently press to seal the edges. Brush the cake with the egg wash, then chill the cake in the fridge for 10–15 minutes. Score the top with a knife to create a pattern. Either leave the edge plain or use a knife to create a scalloped edge. Bake for 35–40 minutes or until golden brown. Let cool before serving.

Vasilopita

SERVES 10

1 cup **unsalted butter**
  at room temperature,
  plus extra for greasing
1 cup **superfine sugar**
zest of 2 large **oranges**
2 tbsp **honey**
4 large **eggs**, lightly beaten
½ cup **all-purpose flour**
1 tsp **baking powder**
¼ tsp **salt**
2 cups **almond flour**

confectioners' sugar,
  for dusting
gold leaf, to decorate
  (optional)

**For the candied
orange peel**
2 large **oranges**
1 cup **superfine sugar**
2–3 tbsp **Cointreau**,
  or to taste

This cake is my version of a classic cake served in Greece on New Year's Day. Like many other traditional cakes, a coin would have been baked into the batter and the person who found it in their slice was said to receive a year's good luck. My favorite way to decorate this simple cake is to top it with candied orange peel and a little edible gold leaf—to start the New Year in style, of course! See page 41 for how to sterilize the jars.

1. Preheat the oven to 350°F. Lightly grease a deep 8in cake pan with parchment paper, greasing the parchment paper too. Put the butter in a large bowl and, using an electric mixer, beat until light and creamy, about 3 minutes. Add the sugar, orange zest, and honey, and beat until light and fluffy, about 5 minutes.

2. Add the eggs, a little a time, beating until fully combined. Sift the flour, baking powder, and salt together in a small bowl and mix in the almonds. Add this mixture to the butter mixture and fold to combine. Pour the batter into the prepared pan and gently level out.

3. Bake for 50–55 minutes until the cake is golden brown and springs backs when lightly touched. If the cake is browning too quickly, put a tent of foil over the top.

4. Meanwhile, prepare the candied peel. Using a vegetable peeler, peel off long strips of orange zest, trying to keep the slices as thin as possible so that you remove as little of the pith as possible. Cut the peel into thin strips and put them in a small pan, then cover with cold water. Put the pan over medium-high heat and bring to a boil.

5. Drain the orange peel, discarding the water, and then repeat this process twice more (this helps to reduce any bitterness in the peel). Put the sugar and ½ cup water into the pan over medium-high heat and bring to a boil. Add the orange zest and then reduce the temperature so that the syrup is at a gentle simmer. Cook the orange, stirring occasionally, for 30–35 minutes or until it turns translucent. Remove from the heat and add the Cointreau. Pour the peel and syrup into a sterilized jar and seal until needed (the candied peel will last for up to three months).

6. Let the cake cool in the pan for 10 minutes before turning onto a wire rack. Use a skewer to make holes all over the top of the cake. Use a pastry brush to coat the cake generously in the reserved orange syrup. Let the cake cool completely then dust with a little confectioners' sugar and decorate with candied orange peel. To make the cake a little more special, I like to add a little edible gold leaf to some of the orange peel.

Hangover Cake

SERVES 8–10

4 tbsp **unsalted butter** at room temperature, plus extra for greasing
¾ cup **all-purpose flour**
1 tsp **baking powder**
2 tsp **ground ginger**
¼ tsp **salt**
½ cup **superfine sugar**
1 large **egg**, lightly beaten
1 tsp **vanilla extract**
¼ cup **plain yogurt**

For the topping
3 tbsp **unsalted butter**
¼ cup **light brown sugar**
about 2 tbsp **dark rum**
3 large **bananas**

New Year's Day is a day of hangovers. We can all admit to enjoying the celebrations a little too much, so this is the perfect hangover cure. It's delicious, fast to make, and full of things that are supposedly good for a hangover: bananas for potassium, ginger to help soothe the stomach, and a shot of rum for the hair of the dog.

1. Preheat the oven to 350°F and lightly grease an 8in cake pan. To make the topping, put the butter in a small pan over medium-high heat. Once the butter has melted, add the sugar and cook until you have a smooth sauce. Take off the heat and add the rum. Taste the caramel, and if you want a stronger flavor, add a little more rum. Pour the caramel into the base of the prepared pan and set aside.

2. In a medium bowl whisk the flour, baking powder, ginger, and salt together to combine, then set aside. Put the butter in a medium bowl and, using an electric mixer, beat until light and creamy, about 3 minutes. Add the sugar and beat together until light and fluffy, about 5 minutes. Add the egg and vanilla, a little at a time, beating until fully combined.

3. Add half the flour mixture, mixing until just combined. Mix in the yogurt, then add the remainder of the flour mixture, stirring just until combined.

4. Peel and slice the bananas into ½in thick slices and spread across the bottom of the prepared pan, then top with the cake batter in an even layer. Bake for 25–30 minutes or until a toothpick inserted into the center comes out clean. Let the cake cool in the pan for 10 minutes before inverting and turning onto a wire rack. It is best served warm.

TIP

This makes a fairly thin cake, so if you want your cake a little taller, double the cake recipe and bake for 40–50 minutes.

Edible Flower Cupcakes

MAKES 12

1½ cups **all-purpose flour**	**edible fresh flowers**, such as
2 tsp **baking powder**	a mixture of **pansies, violas,**
¼ tsp **salt**	and **rose petals**, to decorate
1 cup **unsalted butter**,	
at room temperature	**For the frosting**
1 cup + 2 tbsp **superfine sugar**	1 cup + 2 tbsp **unsalted butter**,
zest of 1 **lemon**	at room temperature
4 large **eggs**, lightly beaten	1 tsp **vanilla bean paste**
1 tsp **vanilla bean paste**	⅓ cup **heavy cream**
½ cup **sour cream**	4⅓ cups **confectioners' sugar**,
	sifted
	pinch of **salt**

There are many flowers that are edible; in fact one of the most frequently used baking ingredients is derived from orchids: vanilla. So the idea of decorating cupcakes with some beautiful flowers shouldn't be that strange. Because the flavor is delicate, to allow them to shine, the cake is just lightly flavored with vanilla and lemon, and the frosting is a beautiful smooth vanilla buttercream. When using flowers with food you need to make sure they haven't been in contact with pesticides, so use a supplier who can guarantee this (see Resources, page 170).

1. Preheat the oven to 325°F. Line a standard 12-cup muffin pan with paper liners. In a medium bowl whisk the flour, baking powder, and salt together to combine, then set aside.

2. Put the butter in a large bowl and, using an electric mixer, beat until smooth and creamy, then add the sugar and lemon zest, and beat until light and fluffy, about 5 minutes. Beat in the eggs and vanilla, a little at a time, beating well after each addition. Add the sour cream and mix until fully combined. Add the flour mixture and fold until fully combined (folding in the flour will help prevent over-mixing).

3. Divide the batter among the liners and bake for 22–25 minutes or until a skewer inserted into one of the cakes comes out clean. Transfer to a wire rack to cool completely.

4. To make the frosting, beat the butter and vanilla bean paste using an electric mixer until light and creamy. With the mixer on medium speed, slowly incorporate the heavy cream. Once light and smooth, slowly incorporate the confectioners' sugar and salt, then beat on high speed until light and fluffy.

5. To decorate the cupcakes, put the buttercream in a piping bag fitted with a large star piping tube and pipe in a spiral starting in the center of a cupcake and working out to the edge. Take the flowers off their stems and place onto the cakes.

TIP

If you are making rose-decorated cakes, add a little rose syrup to the buttercream to add a delicate floral note.

90

Individual Carrot Cakes

MAKES 12

oil spray or melted **butter**, for greasing
2 cups **all-purpose flour**
2 tsp **baking soda**
¼ tsp **salt**
1 tbsp **ground cinnamon**
1 tsp freshly grated **nutmeg**
2 tsp **ground ginger**
4 large **eggs**
1 cup **superfine sugar**
1 cup **light brown sugar**

1 cup **olive oil**
zest of 1 large **orange**, plus extra for decoration
3 cups **carrots**, grated (about 4 carrots)
1⅓ cups **currants**

For the cream cheese glaze
⅔ cup **full-fat cream cheese**
3 cups **confectioners' sugar**
2 tbsp **milk**
1 tsp **vanilla bean paste**

These cakes have a pretty shape, which comes from them being baked in mini Bundt pans. Their flavor reminds me of the carrot cakes my mother used to make; although she was never a fan of cakes made with oil, I think for a carrot cake it gives the perfect texture.

1. Preheat the oven to 350°F and grease 12 mini Bundt pans with oil spray or melted butter. Mix the flour, baking soda, salt, and spices together in a large bowl and set aside.

2. In a medium bowl whisk the eggs, sugars, oil, and orange zest together until combined and smooth. Pour onto the flour mixture, add the grated carrots and currants, and mix together well.

3. Fill the Bundt pans about three-quarters full, and bake for 25–30 minutes or until a skewer inserted into the center of a cake comes out clean and the cake springs back when lightly touched.

4. Let the cakes cool in the pans for 10 minutes before turning onto a wire rack to cool completely. While cooling, make the cream cheese glaze. Put all the ingredients in a bowl and whisk together until smooth. To decorate the cakes, spoon or pipe the glaze onto the cakes and finish with a little grating of orange zest.

TIP

Greasing pans with oil spray is fast and easy, and it covers the pans well. It's especially useful for pans such as Bundt pans. You can now get these sprays at most supermarkets and speciality baking supply shops.

Lemon Tart

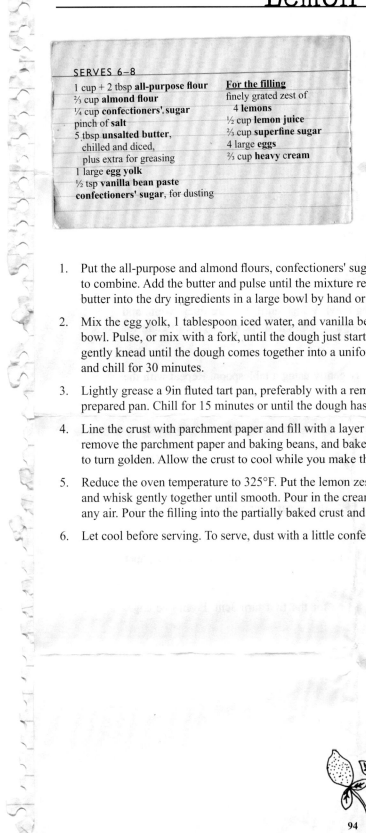

SERVES 6–8

1 cup + 2 tbsp **all-purpose flour**	**For the filling**
⅔ cup **almond flour**	finely grated zest of
¼ cup **confectioners' sugar**	4 **lemons**
pinch of **salt**	½ cup **lemon juice**
5 tbsp **unsalted butter**,	⅔ cup **superfine sugar**
chilled and diced,	4 large **eggs**
plus extra for greasing	⅔ cup **heavy cream**
1 large **egg yolk**	
½ tsp **vanilla bean paste**	
confectioners' sugar, for dusting	

Lemon tarts are one of those classic desserts that haven't really changed much over time, and that's good because a classic lemon tart is a thing of beauty: fresh, zingy, and citrussy—totally delicious. Making this for your mother on Mother's Day will be a real treat—and what a nice way to say thank you to such a wonderful person.

1. Put the all-purpose and almond flours, confectioners' sugar, and salt in the bowl of a food processor and pulse to combine. Add the butter and pulse until the mixture resembles coarse bread crumbs. (Alternatively, rub the butter into the dry ingredients in a large bowl by hand or using a pastry cutter.)

2. Mix the egg yolk, 1 tablespoon iced water, and vanilla bean paste together and add to the food processor or bowl. Pulse, or mix with a fork, until the dough just starts to come together. Transfer to the work surface and gently knead until the dough comes together into a uniform mass. Press into a flat disc, wrap in plastic wrap, and chill for 30 minutes.

3. Lightly grease a 9in fluted tart pan, preferably with a removable bottom. Roll out the dough and line the prepared pan. Chill for 15 minutes or until the dough has firmed up. Preheat the oven to 400°F.

4. Line the crust with parchment paper and fill with a layer of baking beans or rice. Bake for 20 minutes, then remove the parchment paper and baking beans, and bake for another 5–10 minutes or until the crust has started to turn golden. Allow the crust to cool while you make the filling.

5. Reduce the oven temperature to 325°F. Put the lemon zest and juice, sugar, and eggs into a medium bowl and whisk gently together until smooth. Pour in the cream and stir gently to combine, without incorporating any air. Pour the filling into the partially baked crust and bake for 30 minutes or until the filling has just set.

6. Let cool before serving. To serve, dust with a little confectioners' sugar before slicing.

94

Ginger Guinness Cake with Lemon Cream Cheese Frosting

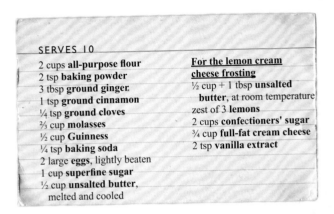

SERVES 10

2 cups **all-purpose flour**
2 tsp **baking powder**
3 tbsp **ground ginger**
1 tsp **ground cinnamon**
¼ tsp **ground cloves**
⅔ cup **molasses**
½ cup **Guinness**
¼ tsp **baking soda**
2 large **eggs**, lightly beaten
1 cup **superfine sugar**
½ cup **unsalted butter,**
   melted and cooled

For the lemon cream cheese frosting
½ cup + 1 tbsp **unsalted butter**, at room temperature
zest of 3 **lemons**
2 cups **confectioners' sugar**
¾ cup **full-fat cream cheese**
2 tsp **vanilla extract**

Guinness is the sort of drink I always picture dads and grandfathers drinking, and so this cake seems perfect for Father's Day. What's more, the good news is that even if you don't like Guinness you will still love the cake, because the main flavor is ginger and the Guinness just helps to give the cake a bit of depth and warmth.

1. Preheat the oven to 350°F. Grease and line two 9in cake pans with parchment paper, greasing the parchment paper too. Combine the flour, baking powder, ginger, cinnamon, and cloves together into a medium bowl and set aside.

2. Put the molasses and Guinness in a medium pan and bring to a boil. Turn off the heat and add the baking soda. The mixture will bubble up; set aside until it settles down. In a medium bowl, whisk the eggs and sugar together until thickened and pale. Drizzle in the melted butter and whisk to combine. Whisk the Guinness mixture into the egg mixture.

3. Sift the flour mixture over the liquid ingredients and gently fold together until combined. Divide equally between the prepared pans and bake for 50–60 minutes or until a toothpick inserted into the center of the cakes comes out clean. Allow the cakes to cool in the pans for 15 minutes before turning onto a wire rack to cool completely.

4. To make the frosting, put the butter and lemon zest in a large bowl and, using an electric mixer, beat until light and smooth, about 5 minutes. Slowly beat in the confectioners' sugar until fully combined, then increase the speed and beat until light and fluffy. Add the cream cheese and vanilla extract and beat until just combined. Do not over-beat at this stage or the frosting will be too thin.

5. To assemble the cake, put the first cake layer on a cardboard cake board or serving plate and cover the top with a thick layer of frosting. Top with the second layer of cake and spread the remaining frosting on the top of the cake.

Espresso Sablés

MAKES ABOUT 30

½ cup + 3 tbsp **unsalted butter**,
  at room temperature
⅓ cup **superfine sugar**
¼ cup **light brown sugar**
2 **large egg yolks**
2 cups **all-purpose flour**,
  plus extra for dusting
2–3 tsp **finely ground coffee**

For the chocolate ganache filling
4oz **dark chocolate**
  (about 70% cocoa solids),
  finely chopped
⅓ cup **heavy cream**
1 tbsp **unsalted butter**,
  softened

When I think of my dad, coffee is one of the things that springs to mind. He has always loved his espresso, but when I was a child I thought it tasted awful even though I loved the smell. Now I love the flavor, and these little sablés taste great and are full of flavor. Serve them with a coffee for the perfect pairing.

1. Put the butter and sugars in the bowl of a food processor and beat until smooth and creamy. Add the egg yolks and pulse until combined. Add the flour and coffee and pulse until the mixture just starts to come together. (Alternatively, beat the butter and sugars using an electric mixer, then beat in the egg yolks. Add the flour and coffee and gently mix until the mixture just comes together.)

2. Transfer the mixture to the work surface and gently knead together, being careful not to overwork it. Wrap the dough in plastic wrap and chill for 30 minutes. Preheat the oven to 350°F and line two baking sheets with parchment paper.

3. Roll out the dough on a lightly floured work surface to ⅛in thick. Using a knife or pizza cutter, cut out about 60 squares of dough about 1¼in wide. Put on the baking sheet and bake for 10–12 minutes or until lightly golden, then transfer to a wire rack to cool completely.

4. To make the filling, put the chocolate in a medium heatproof bowl. Put the cream in a small pan over medium heat and bring just to a boil. Pour the cream over the chocolate and leave for a few minutes before gently stirring together to form a silky smooth ganache. Add the butter and mix until combined. Allow to firm up a little, then put in a piping bag with a small plain piping tip and pipe onto the sablés, then sandwich the cookies together.

Chocolate Peanut Butter Cake

SERVES 12

For the peanut dacquoise
- 2½ tbsp **egg whites** (about 1 large egg)
- 3 tbsp **superfine sugar**
- ¼ cup **salted peanuts**, finely chopped

For the chocolate cremeux layer
- ½ sheet **gelatin**
- 5½oz **dark chocolate** (about 70% cocoa solids), finely chopped
- ½ cup **whole milk**
- ½ cup **heavy cream**
- 2 tbsp **light brown sugar**
- 2 large **egg yolks**
- pinch of **sea salt**

For the caramel filling
- ⅓ cup **granulated sugar**
- ¼ cup **heavy cream**
- pinch of **sea salt**
- 1 tsp **salted butter**, softened

For the peanut butter mousse
- 2 sheets **gelatin**
- 1 cup **smooth peanut butter**
- 2½ cups **heavy cream**
- ½ cup **confectioners' sugar**

To finish
- ¾ cup **heavy cream**, whipped to medium peaks
- **cocoa powder**, for dusting

Peanut butter and chocolate are a well-known and wonderful combination, used here for a rich mousse cake. It's an indulgent dessert to share with lots of people. Although there are several steps, you should find them straightforward to follow, and the recipe uses fairly simple ingredients that are easy to get ahold of.

1. To make this dessert you will need an 8in mousse ring (available from good kitchen suppliers), but if you don't have one and would rather not buy one, you can also use the ring from an 8in springform cake pan. Put the ring onto a flat plate and set aside. Preheat the oven to 225°F and line a baking sheet with parchment paper.

2. Put the egg whites in a clean, grease-free bowl and beat with a hand-held mixer until they form soft peaks. With the mixer still on high, slowly pour in the sugar and continue to beat until the meringue holds stiff and glossy peaks.

3. Gently fold in the chopped peanuts. Using an offset spatula, or the back of a spoon, spread the dacquoise mixture onto the prepared baking sheet in a circular shape just over 8in diameter. Bake for 2 hours or until the meringue is very lightly browned and crisp. Remove from the oven and transfer to a wire rack to cool completely.

4. Press the mousse ring onto the meringue and, using it like a cookie cutter, cut out a disc to fit in the base of the ring. Put the ring and the meringue onto the flat plate and set aside.

5. To make the cremeux layer, put the gelatin in a small bowl and cover with cold water. Put the chocolate in a medium bowl and set aside. Put the milk, cream, and half the sugar in a medium pan over medium heat and bring to a boil. While the liquid is heating, whisk the egg yolks with the remaining sugar and the salt.

6. When the milk mixture has just come to a boil, remove it from the heat and pour half in the egg yolks, whisking to combine. Pour the egg mixture into the pan and put back on the heat. Cook, stirring constantly, until the custard coats the back of a spoon. Pour the custard over the chocolate and let stand for a few minutes. Add the softened gelatin and stir the mixture together until it is smooth and glossy. Pour the chocolate cremeux into the ring and put in the fridge to set.

7. To make the caramel filling, put the sugar in a medium pan over medium heat and cook until dissolved and dark golden brown in color, stopping before it starts to smoke. Remove from the heat and carefully pour in half the cream and add the salt. The mixture will bubble violently, so be careful and go slowly.

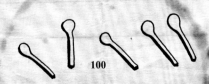

1. Once the mixture has settled, add the remaining cream followed by the butter. If the mixture is lumpy, put it back over low heat and stir until smooth. Pour into a heatproof bowl to cool. Pour the cooled caramel filling over the chocolate layer, leaving a ½in border. Put back into the fridge until needed.

2. To make the peanut butter mousse, put the gelatin in a small bowl and cover with cold water, then set aside for 10 minutes to soften. Put the peanut butter in a small pan and gently warm over low heat so that it becomes more fluid. Add the softened gelatin and whisk to combine.

3. Pour the peanut butter mixture into a large bowl and add the cream and confectioners' sugar, whisking to combine. Chill the mousse mixture for 15–20 minutes, then whisk lightly until the mousse slightly increases in volume. Pour this mousse into the ring and put in the fridge to set.

4. When ready to serve, remove from the fridge and use a blowtorch, or a kitchen towel soaked in hot water and wrung out, to heat the mousse ring to release it from the dessert. To finish, put the whipped cream in a piping bag fitted with a large plain piping tip and pipe a spiral onto the top of the dessert. Dust the cream with a small amount of cocoa powder.

Chocolate & Guinness Bundt Cake

SERVES 12–16

1 cup + 2 tbsp **unsalted butter**,
  plus extra for greasing
  or an oil spray
¾ cup **Guinness**
¾ cup **cocoa powder**
2½ cups **all-purpose flour**
1½ tsp **baking soda**
½ tsp **salt**
2 cups **superfine sugar**
¾ cup **sour cream**
3 large **eggs**

Suprisingly, chocolate and Guinness are a great combination, and used in a chocolate cake it gives a wonderfully deep flavor. The texture of this cake is quite dense and moist. It's not a light cake for a refined afternoon party, but rather a full-flavored and comforting cake.

1. Preheat the oven to 350°F and grease a 6-cup Bundt pan very well—the cake will stick very easily if this pan isn't properly greased; an oil spray is faster and gives a very even coating. Melt the butter in a medium pan. Add the Guinness and cocoa powder, whisking until you have a smooth liquid.

2. In a large bowl, mix together the flour, baking soda, and salt. Add the sugar, sour cream, and eggs to the Guinness mixture and whisk to combine. Pour this over the flour mixture and whisk until you have a smooth batter.

3. Pour the batter into the prepared pan and bake for 40–45 minutes or until the cake springs back when lightly touched; a skewer inserted into the cake will come out with just the odd crumb. Let cool in the pan for about 15 minutes before turning onto a wire rack to cool completely. If the cake is domed, use a serrated knife to level it. Turn the cake upside down onto a serving plate.

4. To make the glaze, put the chocolate in a medium heatproof bowl and set aside. Put the cream in a medium pan set over medium heat and bring just to a boil. Pour in the chocolate and let stand for a few minutes before stirring gently to form a silky smooth ganache. Let cool slightly until it has thickened a little. Pour over the top of the cake, allowing it to drip down the sides.

101

Blackberry & Mint Cake

Sometimes you want a decadent triple layer cake, but at other times you want a cake that can be whipped together in no time—and this is one of those cakes. Although it's easy to make, it's still delicious and beautiful to look at.

SERVES 12

1 cup **unsalted butter** at room temperature, plus extra for greasing	**For the mint frosting**
1¾ cups **self-rising flour**	¾ cup **unsalted butter** at room temperature
2 tsp **baking powder**	⅓ cup **heavy cream**
1 cup plus 2 tbsp **superfine sugar**	3⅓ cups **confectioners' sugar**
4 large **eggs**, lightly beaten	a pinch of **salt**
1–2 tbsp **milk**, if needed	¼–½ tsp **peppermint extract**
3 tbsp **blackberry** or **blackcurrant liqueur** (optional)	**green food coloring** (optional)
1¼ cups **blackberries**	

For the decoration
3½oz **dark chocolate** (about 70% cocoa solids), finely chopped
leaves from 1 bunch of **mint**
¼ cup **blackberry jam**
1¼ cups **blackberries**

TIP

To remove the mint leaves easily, the chocolate needs to be fairly thick. If you want to make the decoration easier, just put the leaves onto the cake without peeling them off, the green will look nice and will add another level of flavor.

1. Preheat the oven to 350°F. Lightly grease and line two 8in cake pans with parchment paper, greasing the parchment too. In a medium bowl whisk the flour and baking powder together, then set aside.

2. Put the butter and sugar in a large bowl and, using an electric mixer, beat together until light and fluffy, about 5 minutes. Add the eggs, a little at a time, beating until fully combined. With the mixer on low, sift in the flour mixture in three additions, mixing until just combined.

3. The cake batter should be a "dropping consistency," which means that if you take a spoonful of batter out of the bowl it should be soft enough to fall easily from the spoon. If the batter is sticking to the spoon for too long, mix in 1–2 tablespoons milk to soften the batter. Add the liqueur and blackberries and gently mix into the batter.

4. Divide the cake batter evenly between the two prepared cake pans and gently level out. Bake for 25–30 minutes or until golden brown and coming away from the edge of the pan; a toothpick inserted into the center of a cake should come out clean. Let cool in the pan for 10 minutes before turning onto a wire rack to cool completely.

5. While the cakes are cooling, make the frosting. Put the butter in a large bowl and, using an electric mixer, beat until light and creamy, about 3 minutes. Slowly incorporate the cream and beat until fully combined. Add the confectioners' sugar, a little at a time, and once fully combined add the salt. Beat on high speed until the frosting is light and fluffy. Add the peppermint extract and coloring, if using, and beat to combine.

6. To make the decoration, melt the chocolate in a heatproof bowl set over a pan of gently simmering water, making sure the bottom of the bowl doesn't touch the water. Put the mint leaves on a parchment-lined baking sheet. Using a pastry brush, paint one side of each leaf with the melted chocolate. Put the tray in the fridge until the chocolate is set.

7. To assemble the cake, put one of the cake layers on a cardboard cake round or a serving plate. Top with half the frosting and spread evenly across the cake. Top with a thin layer of blackberry jam and then put the second cake layer on top. Spread the remaining buttercream over the top of the cake and sprinkle with the blackberries. Remove the mint leaves from the fridge and carefully peel off the leaves, leaving you with chocolate mint leaves. Put these randomly over the top of the cake.

103

Jack-O'-Lantern Cakes

MAKES 4 CAKES (EACH SERVING 2 PEOPLE)

⅔ cup **unsalted butter**, melted and cooled, plus extra for greasing .
1½ cups **all-purpose flour**
2 tsp **baking powder**
½ tsp **salt**
2 tsp **ground cinnamon**
1 tsp **pumpkin pie spice**
¼ tsp **ground cloves**
7oz **pumpkin purée** (see Tips)
⅓ cup plus 1 tbsp **plain yogurt**
1 cup **light brown sugar**

2 large **eggs**
1 tsp **vanilla bean paste**

For the cream cheese frosting
1 cup + 2 tbsp **unsalted butter** at room temperature
4½ cups **confectioners' sugar**, sifted
1¾ cups **full-fat cream cheese**
1 tsp **vanilla extract**
orange gel coloring
a little **black royal icing**

These little cakes, flavored with pumpkin, are perfect for a Halloween party. Once decorated they look just like mini Jack-o'-lanterns, and rather adorable they are too. You will need two mini bundlette trays to make the cakes, or you can make a single cake (see Tips).

1. Preheat the oven to 350°F and grease eight mini bundlette cups. In a medium bowl, whisk together the flour, baking powder, salt, and spices, then set aside.

2. In a large bowl add the pumpkin purée with the yogurt, sugar, eggs, vanilla paste, and butter, then mix together until evenly combined. Sift the flour mixture over the liquid ingredients and gently fold together until the dry ingredients are incorporated (don't beat the batter or the cake will be tough).

3. Divide the mixture between the prepared molds, filling about half-full, and bake for 20–25 minutes until the cakes are risen and golden brown, and a skewer inserted into the center of a cake comes out clean. Allow the cakes to cool in the pan for 10 minutes before turning onto a wire rack to cool completely.

4. To make the frosting, put the butter in a large bowl and, using an electric mixer, beat until light and smooth, about 3 minutes. Slowly beat in the confectioners' sugar until fully combined, then increase the speed and beat until light and fluffy. Add the cream cheese and vanilla extract, and beat until just combined. Do not over-beat or the frosting will be too thin. Color the frosting with a very small amount of orange gel coloring and mix to combine.

5. To assemble, use a serrated knife to remove the top of each cake to make it flat. Sandwich two cakes together with a little frosting, and then use a small offset spatula or the back of a spoon to coat the cakes in a layer of frosting. If you like, you can pipe a face on the lanterns using a little black royal icing and a small plain piping tip in the piping bag. To make the stems for the pumpkins, roll a small amount of green fondant into a thin sausage and cut a short piece for each cake, placing it on the top.

TIP

If you prefer, you can make a single cake using a 1lb loaf pan, although it won't have the same pumpkin shape. Bake for 50 minutes at 350°F.

TIP

You can use canned pumpkin if you can find it or use 7oz pumpkin boiled or steamed until tender, then drained and puréed using a blender.

Classic Christmas Cake

SERVES 15-20

1½ cups **golden raisins**	1¼ cups **all-purpose flour**
1½ cups **raisins**	1¼ cups **almond flour**
1½ cups **currants**	¼ tsp **salt**
4oz **mixed peel**	1½ tsp **ground cinnamon**
4oz **glacé cherries**	1½ tsp **mixed spice**
zest of 1 **lemon**	1 cup + 2 tbsp **superfine sugar**
zest of 1 **orange**	5 large **eggs**, lightly beaten
¼ cup **brandy**	
1 cup **unsalted butter**	
at room temperature,	
plus extra for greasing	

For the almond paste	
1½ cups **confectioners' sugar**	1 tsp **almond extract**,
3½ cups **almond flour**	or to taste
¾ cup + 2 tbsp **superfine**	1 tbsp **rum**
sugar, plus extra for dusting	¼ cup **apricot jam**, sieved
1 large **egg**	**For the icing**
1 large **egg white**	3¾ cups **confectioners'**
	sugar or 2¾lb **white fondant**

In England, the smell of a fruity Christmas cake baking means the season has really started. It fills the kitchen and the house with a beautifully warming aroma, which to most people is the smell of Christmas. To decorate the cake you can either use royal icing, which is my preference, or you can cover it with fondant. Either way, if you are making the cake weeks or months in advance, store the cake undecorated and well wrapped in plastic wrap, then cover it in almond paste and icing nearer the time.

1. The night before you want to make the cake, put the fruits, zests, and brandy in a large bowl and mix together. Cover with plastic wrap and let soak overnight.

2. The next day, preheat the oven to 300°F, then grease and triple-line a deep 10in cake pan with parchment paper. In a medium bowl whisk the flour, almonds, salt, and spices together to combine, then set aside.

3. Put the butter and sugar in a large bowl and, using an electric mixer, beat until light and fluffy, about 5 minutes. Beat in the eggs, a little at a time, beating until fully combined. With the mixer on low, add the flour mixture, a large spoonful at a time, mixing until just combined. Using a large spatula or metal spoon, fold in the fruit.

4. Scrape the batter into the prepared pan and bake for 1 hour. Reduce the temperature to 225°F and bake for another 2 hours or until a toothpick inserted into the center comes out clean. If the cake is browning too quickly, put a tent of foil over the top. Allow the cake to cool completely in the pan before removing.

5. To make the almond paste, sift the confectioners' sugar and almonds into a large bowl, to break up any lumps. Add the superfine sugar and mix to combine. Pour in the egg and egg white, almond extract, and rum and, using a wooden spoon, mix to form a stiff dough. Wrap in plastic wrap and chill until needed.

6. To assemble the cake, put the apricot jam in a small pan with 1 tablespoon water and cook until the jam is bubbling. Brush the cake all over with the jam, which will act as a glue for the almond paste.

7. Divide the almond paste into two portions. Dust the work surface with a little confectioners' sugar and roll the first portion of almond paste into a strip to fit around the cake, but very slightly taller than the cake. Gently press around the outside of the cake, using the palms of your hands to smooth the paste around the cake.

8. Take the second portion of almond paste and roll out into a 10½in circle to fit onto the top. Put the paste onto the cake, applying gentle pressure to stick it to the surface. Using the palms of your hands, gently press the edges of the two pieces of almond paste together and smooth them together to eliminate any seal. Allow the cake to dry overnight before icing.

9. If using royal icing, put the confectioners' sugar in a large bowl with ¼ cup water. Using a wooden spoon, beat together until it forms a thick and smooth paste. Pour the icing on top of the cake and, using an

offset spatula, spread the icing across the top and sides of the cake. To finish, you can use the spatula to spike the icing, giving it the look of snow, if you like. If you want a smooth finish, warm the offset spatula in a bowl of boiling water, then dry with paper towels and use the hot spatula to smooth out the icing.

10. If using fondant, take the white fondant and knead it until pliable. The colder the fondant the longer it will need to be worked with to soften it. Lightly dust the work surface with a little confectioners' sugar and roll out the fondant until it is large enough to cover the cake. The easiest way to do this is to take a piece of string and use it as a guide. Drape it over the cake and grip it where it meets the table. Lift the string from the cake and use this as a measure for your fondant. Brush the almond paste with a little water to make the surface slightly tacky. Using the flats of your hands and arms, drape the fondant over the cake, and use the palms of your hands to smooth the top, applying a gentle pressure. Carefully work your way around the cake, gently smoothing the fondant onto the sides, and trimming off the excess.

11. You can then decorate the cake as you wish. My preference is to wrap the cake in a strip of ribbon and then top with a few store-bought decorations my family has had for years.

Modern Christmas Cake

SERVES 12

2¼ cups **all-purpose flour**
⅓ cup **cornstarch**
4½ tsp **baking powder**
½ tsp **salt**
1 cup **unsalted butter** at room temperature, plus extra for greasing
1¼ cups **superfine sugar**
2 tsp **vanilla extract**
4 medium **eggs**, lightly beaten
¾ cup **whole milk**

½ cup **cranberry sauce**
holly leaf decorations (optional)

For the sugared cranberries
½ cup **superfine sugar**, plus extra for coating
1 **cinnamon stick**
½ cup **cranberries**

For the white chocolate Italian meringue buttercream
5½oz **white chocolate**, finely chopped
1¼ cups **superfine sugar**
6 medium **egg whites**
2 cups **unsalted butter** at room temperature

If you're one of the many people who really dislikes fruit cake, here is something a little different. I have kept the frosting white so that it resembles the more traditional Christmas cake, but it is actually flavored with white chocolate and cranberries. The cake has a real elegance, because it is decorated with sugared cranberries and holly, a perfect centerpiece for the Christmas table.

1. First make the sugared cranberries. Put the sugar in a small pan with ⅓ cup water and bring to a boil. Reduce the temperature to medium and cook the syrup at a simmer for 5 minutes or until the sugar has fully dissolved. Add the cinnamon stick and remove the pan from the heat. Put the cranberries in a container with a tight-fitting lid and, once the syrup has cooled slightly, pour it over the cranberries and seal the container. Cool, then pop in the fridge overnight.

2. Remove the cranberries from the fridge and drain thoroughly. Roll them in superfine sugar and set aside to dry for 2 hours. Preheat the oven to 350°F, then grease and line three 8in cake pans with parchment paper, greasing the parchment too.

112

3. In a medium bowl whisk the flour, cornstarch, baking powder, and salt together to combine, then set aside. Put the butter in a large bowl and, using an electric mixer, beat on medium-high speed until smooth and light. Add the sugar and beat until light and fluffy, about 5 minutes. Add the vanilla and mix to combine. With the mixer on medium speed, add the eggs, a little at a time, beating until fully combined before adding more. With the mixer on low, sift in the flour mixture alternating with the milk, in three additions starting and finishing with the flour.

4. Divide the batter evenly among the prepared pans and bake for 30–35 minutes or until the cakes are golden brown and spring back when lightly touched. Allow the cakes to cool in the pans for 10 minutes before turning onto a wire rack to cool completely.

5. To make the buttercream, melt the white chocolate in a heatproof bowl set over a pan of gently simmering water, making sure the bottom of the bowl doesn't touch the water. Remove from the heat and let cool.

6. Put ½ cup water and the sugar in a pan over medium heat, and have a sugar thermometer ready. Put the egg whites in a clean, grease-free bowl (this is best done using a freestanding electric mixer). As the syrup reaches about 225°F, start whisking on high speed. Cook until the syrup registers 250°F, then remove from the heat and, with the mixer still running, pour the syrup in a slow stream down the side of the bowl containing the whites, avoiding the beaters. Continue whisking on high speed until the meringue is at room temperature.

7. With the mixer on medium-high speed, add the butter, a few pieces at a time, beating until fully combined. When adding the butter it can sometimes look curdled, if this happens, don't worry, just keep mixing and eventually it will smooth out again forming a light buttercream. Pour in the melted and cooled white chocolate and mix to combine fully.

8. To assemble the cake, put the first cake layer on a cardboard cake round or a serving plate and top with a layer of the buttercream. Spread half the cranberry sauce on top, leaving a ¾in border. Top with the second cake layer and repeat as before, then top with the last layer of cake. Spread the remaining buttercream across the top and sides of the cake. Top with the sugared cranberries and some holly leaves.

Coconut & Raspberry Cake

SERVES 12

1 cup **unsalted butter**
  at room temperature,
  plus extra for greasing
2¼ cups **all-purpose flour**
⅓ cup **cornstarch**
4½ tsp **baking powder**
½ tsp **salt**
2 cups **superfine sugar**
2 tsp **vanilla extract**
5 medium **egg whites**
½ cup plus 1 tbsp **whole milk**
½ cup plus 1 tbsp **coconut milk**

For the coconut crème mousseline
5 large **egg yolks**
1 cup **superfine sugar**
⅓ cup **all-purpose flour**
1⅔ cups **coconut milk**
⅓ cup plus 1 tbsp **whole milk**
2 cups **unsalted butter**
  at room temperature
1 tsp **vanilla bean paste**
2 tsp **coconut extract**,
  or to taste

To finish
⅔ cup **raspberry jam**
2¾ cups **sweetened shredded coconut**

I know coconut comes across as tropical, summery even, but a cake that's covered in coconut just looks really Christmassy to me—it looks like freshly fallen snow. The frosting for this cake is very different from regular buttercream or frostings. It has a base of thickened coconut custard, to which you add butter, and this forms a beautifully light crème mousseline. Because the crème isn't very sweet, my preference is to cover the cake with sweetened shredded coconut, but if you prefer, you can, of course, just use unsweetened.

1. To make the mousseline, in a large bowl whisk the egg yolks, sugar, and flour together to form a thick paste. Put the coconut milk and whole milk in a large pan over medium-high heat and bring to a boil. Remove from the heat and pour half the milk mixture into the egg mixture, whisking to combine.

2. Pour the egg mixture into the pan and whisk to combine. Put the pan back on the heat and whisk continuously until the mixture boils, then whisk for another 3 minutes—the custard should be very thick.

3. Pour the thickened custard back into the bowl and allow it to cool for a few minutes. Add the softened butter, vanilla bean paste, and coconut extract. Whisk to combine, then press some plastic wrap to the surface and chill for 50–60 minutes or until the mousseline has the texture of buttercream.

4. Preheat the oven to 350°F, then grease and line three 8in cake pans with parchment paper, greasing the parchment paper too. In a medium bowl whisk the flour, cornstarch, baking powder, and salt together to combine, then set aside. Put the butter in a large bowl and, using an electric mixer, beat on medium-high speed until smooth and light, about 3 minutes. Add the sugar and beat until light and fluffy, about 5 minutes. Add the vanilla and mix to combine. With the mixer on medium, add the egg whites, a little at a time, beating until fully combined before adding more. Mix together the milk and coconut milk. With the mixer on low, add the flour mixture to the butter mixture in three additions, alternating with the milks, and starting and finishing with the flour.

5. Divide the batter evenly among the prepared pans and bake for 30–35 minutes or until the cakes spring back when lightly touched. Allow the cakes to cool in the pans for 10 minutes before turning onto a wire rack to cool completely.

6. To assemble the cake, put the first cake layer onto a cardboard cake round or a serving plate and top with a layer of the crème mousseline. Spread half the jam over the mousseline and top with a second layer of cake. Repeat the process. Spread the remaining mousseline over the top and sides of the cake, then coat the whole cake in the shredded coconut.

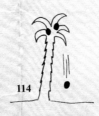

114

Black Forest Roulade

SERVES 8

butter, for greasing
½ cup **all-purpose flour**,
  plus extra for dusting
4 large **eggs**
½ cup **superfine sugar**
½ cup **cocoa powder**,
  plus extra for dusting
2 tbsp **unsalted butter**,
  melted and cooled

For the filling
1 cup **cherries**, pitted
  and halved
about 3 tbsp **kirsch**
1 cup **heavy cream**
½ cup **cherry jam**

For the ganache topping
⅓ cup **heavy cream**
3½oz **dark chocolate**
  (about 70% cocoa solids),
  finely chopped

Ever since I have known my boyfriend, I have made him whatever cake he wants for his birthday. This past year he asked for something with the classic Black Forest flavors of chocolate, cherries, and cream. Since we wanted something quick to make, this roulade was perfect, as it can be whipped up in no time—it will probably be gone in no time too, just what you need during a busy festive period.

1. Preheat the oven to 350°F, then grease and line a 10½ × 15in high-sided baking sheet or brownie pan with parchment paper. Grease the parchment paper and dust with flour, tapping out any excess. Put the eggs and sugar in a heatproof bowl set over a pan of gently simmering water, making sure the bottom of the bowl doesn't touch the water. Whisk constantly until the sugar has dissolved and the mixture is just warm to the touch.

2. Remove the bowl from the pan and, using an electric mixer, beat for 5 minutes on high speed, then reduce the speed to medium and beat for another 3 minutes. By this stage the mixture should have tripled in volume, and when the beaters are lifted from the bowl they should form a slowly dissolving ribbon.

3. Sift in the flour and cocoa and gently fold together, making sure that all the dry ingredients are combined but trying to keep as much volume as possible. Take a large spoonful of the batter and add it to the melted butter, then mix together (this will lighten the butter and help to incorporate it into the batter). Gently fold this into the batter.

4. Pour the batter into the prepared pan and very gently level out. Bake for 15 minutes or until the cake has risen; a skewer inserted into the center should come out clean. Let cool in the pan for 10 minutes before turning onto a wire rack to cool completely.

5. While the cake is baking, make the filling. Put the cherries in a small bowl, pour in 3 tablespoons kirsch, and allow to macerate.

6. When ready to assemble, whisk the cream until it holds medium-firm peaks. Drain the cherries from the kirsch and use the liquid to brush across the cake, adding a little extra kirsch if needed. Brush the cake with a thin layer of cherry jam, and then spread the cream evenly over the cake. Scatter the cherries across the cream.

7. Carefully roll the cake into a log, along the short edge, and place onto a serving plate. To finish the cake, put the cream for the ganache in a small pan over medium heat and just bring to a boil. Put the chocolate in a medium heatproof bowl and pour in the hot cream. Let stand for a few minutes before stirring gently to form a silky smooth ganache, then let stand until it has thickened. Spread the ganache all over the roulade and dust with a little cocoa powder to finish.

Stollen

MAKES 1 LARGE LOAF

1 cup **whole milk**

7 tbsp **unsalted butter**

3 cups **bread flour**, .
plus extra for dusting

1 tsp **pumpkin pie spice**

¼ cup **superfine sugar**

1 tsp **salt**

¼oz **instant yeast**

1 large **egg**

zest of 1 large **lemon**

5½oz **mixed dried fruit**

¼ cup **mixed candied fruit**

¼ cup **almonds**, roughly
chopped

oil, for greasing

7oz **marzipan**

3½ tbsp **unsalted butter**,
melted

confectioners' sugar,
for dusting

Many countries across the world have unique baking traditions at Christmastime. The Germans have stollen, a sweet, fruity bread dough with marzipan running through the center. Although not difficult to make, stollen does take a little effort, and as such I think it makes a great gift during the festive period.

1. Line a baking sheet with parchment paper. Put the milk and butter in a small pan over low heat and heat until the butter has melted. Allow the mixture to stand until it is just lukewarm.

2. In a large bowl, mix the flour, mixed spice, sugar, salt, and yeast together. Add the milk mixture and the egg and mix together with a wooden spoon or your hands to form a soft dough. Lightly flour the work surface and transfer the dough to it. Knead the dough for 10 minutes or until smooth and elastic.

3. Flatten the dough and sprinkle with the lemon zest, dried fruit, candied fruit, and chopped almonds, and knead to distribute evenly. Put the dough in a lightly oiled bowl and cover with plastic wrap. Put the bowl in a warm place and let rise for 1 hour or until doubled in size.

4. Transfer the dough to the floured work surface and lightly knead to knock out some of the air. Press or roll into a 10 × 14in rectangle. Roll the marzipan into a 10in long log and put it in the center of the dough. Lightly brush the edges of the dough with water and fold the dough over the marzipan, then press together to seal. Put the stollen onto the prepared baking sheet. Lightly cover with plastic wrap and let rise for 30 minutes or until doubled in size. Meanwhile, preheat the oven to 375°F.

5. Brush the stollen all over with half the melted butter. Bake for 35–40 minutes or until browned and the stollen sounds hollow when tapped underneath. Transfer to a wire rack to cool for 5 minutes, then brush the loaf with the remaining melted butter and dust with confectioners' sugar. Let cool.

Buche de Noel

SERVES 10

For the chocolate mousse
1 cup good-quality **milk
    chocolate**, finely chopped
2½ cups **heavy cream**

**For the hazelnut
dacquoise base**
⅓ cup **egg whites** (about
    1½ large eggs)
⅓ cup + 1 tbsp **superfine sugar**
⅔ cup finely chopped **hazelnuts**
a pinch of **salt**

**For the chocolate
crunch layer**
3½ oz good-quality **milk
    chocolate**
1 cup **Nutella**
1¾ cups **crispy rice cereal**

**For the caramelized
pear filling**
3 tsp **unsalted butter** .
1½ tbsp **light brown sugar**
2 large **Bosc pears,**
    peeled, cored, and diced

For the glaze
4½oz **dark chocolate**
    (about 70% cocoa solids),
    finely chopped
1 cup **heavy cream**
3 tbsp **corn syrup**

hazelnuts and **edible gold
    powder**, to decorate

I know this recipe has many steps and a long list of ingredients, but I do hope you will give it a try, because all the stages are fairly easy; it just takes time to construct. Imagine how happy your guests will be when you present them with this amazing Parisian-style buche de noel, or yule log, as we would call it. To make this dessert you will need a 10 x 3 x 3 stainless steel U-shaped terrine mold (also called a buche de noel mold). Alternatively, you could make this in a standard 9 x 4in loaf pan, but the cake won't have the same shape. You also need time, so make this on a day that you can dedicate to baking.

1. For the chocolate mousse, melt 6oz of the milk chocolate in a heatproof bowl set over a pan of gently simmering water, making sure the bottom of the bowl doesn't touch the water. Remove from the heat and let cool. Pour 1⅓ cups of the heavy cream into a large bowl and whisk until the mixture barely holds soft peaks.

2. Pour the cooled melted chocolate into the cream and whisk until the mixture is light but holds stiff peaks. Fill a 10 × 3 × 3in stainless steel U-shaped terrine mold with this mousse mixture, leveling it evenly. Use the rounded tip of an offset spatula to make a U-shaped depression along the center of the mold. (This will be filled with pear later.) Wrap the mold in plastic wrap and freeze for 3 hours or until firm.

3. To make the dacquoise, preheat the oven to 225°F and line a baking sheet with parchment paper. Put the egg whites in a clean, grease-free bowl and, using an electric mixer, beat until they form soft peaks. With the mixer still on high, slowly pour in the sugar and continue to beat until the meringue holds stiff with glossy peaks.

4. Gently fold in the chopped hazelnuts and salt. Using an offset spatula or the back of a spoon, spread the dacquoise mixture onto the prepared baking sheet in a rectangular shape just bigger than the terrine mold. Bake for 2 hours or until the meringue is very lightly browned and crisp. Remove from the oven and transfer to a wire rack to cool completely.

5. To make the chocolate crunch layer, melt the chocolate and Nutella in the microwave or in a heatproof bowl set over a pan of gently simmering water. Remove from the heat and let cool slightly, then add the crispy rice cereal and mix to combine. Spread this mixture in an even layer over the cooled dacquoise.

6. To make the pear filling, melt the butter in a medium frying pan over medium heat and add the sugar. Cook for a few minutes until the mixture is bubbling. Add the diced pears and cook, stirring occasionally, for 3–5 minutes or until the pears are caramelized and slightly softened. Pour the pears and any remaining caramel into a small bowl, then cover and set aside until needed. (You can make the pear mixture a day ahead, then cover it with plastic wrap and chill, if you like.)

121

7. Remove the mold from the freezer and take off the plastic wrap. Fill the U-shaped depression with the caramelized pears, trying to add as little caramel as possible. Make another batch of mousse with the remaining ingredients and cover the pear with this batch. Leave a small amount of space in the mold for the final layers.

8. Turn the mold onto the dacquoise and crunch layers. Firmly press the mold down onto the dacquoise, using the mold edges like a cookie cutter. Remove the excess mixture from around the outside of the mold and then wrap the mold in plastic wrap and freeze for at least another 3 hours.

9. Remove the mold from the freezer and invert it onto a wire rack set over a rimmed baking sheet. Using a blowtorch, or a very hot cloth, heat the outside of the mold to release the buche. To make the glaze, melt the chocolate, cream, and corn syrup in a small pan over low heat. Once smooth and shiny, remove from the heat and let cool slightly.

10. To finish the buche, pour the glaze evenly over the mousse, making sure to cover the sides as well as the top. Using a large offset spatula, gently move the buche off the wire rack and onto a serving plate, then transfer to the fridge for a few hours before serving; this will allow the mousse to soften and all the textures to be perfect for eating. (Once fully assembled, the buche will keep well in the fridge for two days.) To decorate, cover a few hazelnuts in edible gold powder and scatter across the top of the dessert.

Figgy Pudding

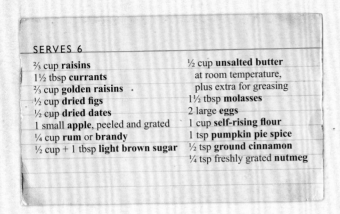

SERVES 6

⅔ cup **raisins**
1½ tbsp **currants**
⅔ cup **golden raisins** .
½ cup **dried figs**
½ cup **dried dates**
1 small **apple**, peeled and grated
¼ cup **rum** or **brandy**
½ cup + 1 tbsp **light brown sugar**

½ cup **unsalted butter**
  at room temperature,
  plus extra for greasing
1½ tbsp **molasses**
2 large **eggs**
1 cup **self-rising flour**
1 tsp **pumpkin pie spice**
½ tsp **ground cinnamon**
¼ tsp freshly grated **nutmeg**

In the Christmas song "We wish You a Merry Christmas" most kids enjoy it when they get to the line where they demand to be brought some figgy pudding—the classic British Christmas dish. My version is lighter than the usual normal Christmas pudding, it isn't stodgy but it still has a boozy flavor. This version is very easy to make and, as it isn't a traditional one, I wouldn't recommend storing for months, it really is best served within a couple days of making.

1. The night before you want to make the pudding, put the raisins, currants, and golden raisins in a medium bowl. Chop the figs and dates so that they are roughly the same size as the rest of the dried fruit. Add to the bowl with the grated apple. Pour in the rum or brandy and mix to combine. Cover the bowl with plastic wrap and set aside overnight to soak.

2. The next day, put the sugar, butter, and molasses in a medium bowl and beat together until light and fluffy, about 5 minutes. Add the eggs, one at a time, beating until fully combined before adding the next. Sift the flour and spices over the butter mixture and fold to combine. Add the fruit and stir until evenly combined.

3. Grease a 1-liter pudding bowl with softened butter, and then scrape the batter into the bowl, pressing it in firmly. Cut a large piece of foil and make a fold in the middle to create a pleat. Cover the basin with the foil and secure by tying a piece of kitchen string around the bowl.

4. Put a small plate upside down in a large pan and put the bowl on top. Fill the pan with enough water to come halfway up the pudding basin, then cover with a lid. Place over high heat and bring the water to a boil. Reduce the temperature so that the water is at a gentle simmer, and cook the pudding for 2 hours. Remove the pan from the heat and carefully remove the pudding. To serve, unwrap and invert onto a serving plate.

MATTY STARTING YOUNG

Christmas Tree Decoration Cookies

MAKES 25

3 cups **all-purpose flour**,
  plus extra for dusting
½ tsp **salt**
1 cup **superfine sugar**
1 tsp **pumpkin pie spice**
½ tsp **ground cinnamon**
¼ tsp freshly grated **nutmeg**
1 cup **unsalted butter**
1 large **egg**
1 large **egg yolk**
1 tsp **vanilla bean paste**

For the royal icing decoration
3¾ cups **confectioners' sugar**
gel food colorings (optional)

There is something very satisfying about making the decorations for your own Christmas tree or even making a batch of these cookies as a gift for friends or family. If you want the cookies to last longer, you can also make them with the dough for my Gingerbread House on page 128.

1. Line two baking sheets with parchment paper. Put the flour, salt, sugar, and spices in the bowl of a food processor and pulse to combine. Add the butter and pulse until the mixture resembles coarse bread crumbs. (Alternatively, mix the dry ingredients in a large bowl and rub the butter into the flour by hand or using a pastry cutter.)

2. Add the egg, yolk, and vanilla paste and pulse (or stir) until the mixture just comes together. Transfer to a lightly floured work surface and gently knead together until uniform. Divide the dough in half and wrap in plastic wrap, then chill for about 1 hour.

3. Working with one half of the dough at a time, roll out to a thickness of ¼in. Cut out as many shapes as possible using Christmas cookie cutters. Re-roll the scraps to cut out more cookies. Lift the cookies off the surface with a spatula and place onto the prepared baking sheets. Chill for 15–20 minutes. Preheat the oven to 350°F.

4. Use a skewer to press a hole into the cookies—this will be used to thread the ribbon to hang the cookies. Bake the cookies for 13–15 minutes or until the edges turn golden. Let cool on the baking sheets for 10 minutes before transferring to a wire rack to cool completely.

5. To make the royal icing, put the confectioners' sugar in a large bowl with ¼ cup water and mix together until you have a thick, barely pourable, paste. Divide the icing between two bowls and add 1–2 teaspoons water to one bowl, then mix well. This icing should be slightly thinner than the first mixture.

6. Depending on how many styles of cookie you want to make, you can divide the icings into smaller batches to color them as you wish. To add the color, use a toothpick to add just a little, then stir to combine evenly. To decorate the cookies, put the thicker icing into a piping bag fitted with a thin piping tube. Pipe around the outside of the cookies; this will act as a barrier to prevent the icing from running off the edges. Make sure to pipe around the hole for the ribbon as well. Allow this to set for a few minutes.

7. Put the slightly runnier icing into a piping bag fitted with a slightly wider piping tube and fill the cookie with the icing. You don't need to pipe a layer over the whole cookie, just give it a rough coating and then use a toothpick to level out the icing and encourage it into any corners. To get a very clean finish, gently shake the cookie—this will remove any cocktail-stick marks. Allow the icing to set overnight. Insert a thin ribbon through the hole and tie it into a loop. The cookies can now be hung on the Christmas tree.

124

Snickerdoodles

MAKES 24

2½ cups **all-purpose flour**
2 tsp **baking powder**
1 tsp **salt**
1 cup **unsalted butter**
   at room temperature
1 cup **superfine sugar**
½ cup **light brown sugar**
2 large **eggs**
1 tsp **vanilla extract**

For the coating
¼ cup **superfine sugar**
3 tsp **ground cinnamon**

For years, I thought snickerdoodles had something to do with the chocolate bar and was expecting something with chocolate, peanuts, and caramel, but these classic American cookies are a lot simpler than that. A delicious buttery cookie, crisp on the outside and soft on the inside rolled in cinnamon sugar—absolutely wonderful!

1. Preheat the oven to 350°F and line two baking sheets with parchment paper. In a medium bowl, whisk the flour, baking powder, and salt together to combine, then set aside. To make the coating, in a small bowl mix the sugar and cinnamon together.

2. Put the butter and sugars in a large bowl and, using an electric mixer, beat together until light and fluffy, about 5 minutes. Add the eggs and vanilla, a little at time, beating until fully combined. Add the flour mixture in three additions, beating until just combined.

3. Using a cookie or ice-cream scoop, divide the dough in half. Take one half of the dough and divide it into 12 equal-sized balls (each ball should weigh about 1½oz—a large tablespoonful of dough). Roll the cookies in the cinnamon sugar and put six on each baking sheet about 2in apart.

4. Bake for 10–12 minutes or until golden around the edges but still soft in the middle. Let cool on the baking sheets for a few minutes before transferring to a wire rack to cool completely. Repeat with the remaining cookie dough.

SILLY MONKEYS HELEN AND GEORGE

Lebkuchen

⅔ cup **honey**
⅔ cup **molasses**
1 cup **light brown sugar**
2 large **eggs**
3½ cups **all-purpose flour**
2 tsp **baking powder**
1 tsp **baking soda**
1 tbsp **ground ginger**
2 tsp **mixed spice**
1 tsp **ground cinnamon**

½ tsp freshly grated **nutmeg**
¼ tsp **ground cloves**
a large pinch of freshly
 ground **black pepper**

For the glaze
¾ cup **confectioners' sugar**
juice of 1 **lemon**

I have to admit that I love the lebkuchen you can buy in foil bags at the supermarket at Christmastime—they are delightfully chewy and spicy. Making a homemade version is actually really easy, so much so that I won't be buying them anymore.

1. Put the honey, molasses, and sugar in a medium pan over medium heat. Stir until the mixture is liquid and the sugar has dissolved. Remove from the heat and let cool slightly. Add the eggs and mix to combine. Put all the dry ingredients in a large bowl and whisk together. Pour in the liquid ingredients and mix together until you have a stiff dough. Cover the bowl with plastic wrap and chill for 4 hours or until firm.

2. Preheat the oven to 350°F and line two baking sheets with parchment paper. Form the dough into 24 tablespoon-sized balls and put 12 balls onto each pan. Flatten each cookie slightly and bake for 10 minutes or until set and lightly browned around the outside. Put the cookies onto a wire rack to cool slightly.

3. To make the glaze, mix the confectioners' sugar and lemon juice in a small bowl until smooth (the mixture should be thin and pourable). While the cookies are still slightly warm, dip them into the glaze, allowing any excess to drip off. Allow the glaze to dry before serving.

TIP

As with all gingerbread recipes, these cookies taste better after a day or two.

127

Gingerbread House

MAKES 1 HOUSE

¾ cup + 2 tbsp **unsalted butter**
1 cup **light brown sugar**
¼ cup **corn syrup**
3½ cups **self-rising flour**,
   plus extra for dusting
1 tbsp **ground ginger**
2 tsp **mixed spice**
1 tsp **ground cinnamon**
½ tsp freshly grated **nutmeg**

For the decoration
4 cups **confectioners'**
   sugar
a selection of small **candies**
shredded coconut

Making a gingerbread house is such a fun thing to do with kids (or without, if you're a big kid like me), and making them fills the house with a wonderful Christmassy smell of ginger and spices. I have provided a template for a house (see page 166) but you could always make your own and go wild with the decoration.

1. Preheat the oven to 350°F and line two baking sheets with parchment paper. In a large pan over medium heat, melt the butter, sugar, and corn syrup together. Meanwhile, sift the remaining ingredients together in a medium bowl. Remove the pan from the heat and pour the butter mixture over the dry ingredients, then mix together using a wooden spoon to form a stiff dough.

2. Lightly dust the work surface with flour and roll out the dough until it is ¼in thick. Using the house template (see page 166), cut out the house pieces and gently transfer to the prepared baking sheets. Bake for 15–20 minutes or until set around the edges and lightly browned. Cool on the baking sheets for 10 minutes, then transfer to wire racks to cool completely before using to build your house.

3. To assemble the house you will need a board, such as a round or square cardboard cake drum, but you could also use a flat plate or even a cake stand. To make the icing, which will act as glue, put the confectioners' sugar in a large bowl and add ¼ cup water. Using a wooden spoon, beat together to form a thick paste. Put the royal icing in a piping bag fitted with a medium plain piping tip. Pipe strips of royal icing onto the edges of the gingerbread pieces.

4. One by one, stick the wall pieces together. To support the house while you build it, put cans next to each wall. Let the royal icing dry for at least 1 hour before you attach the roof to the house. Add the roof pieces, supporting the roof edges with cans or books to keep the pieces from sliding off while the icing dries.

5. To decorate, use the remaining royal icing to pipe tiles on the roof and to fix candy all over the house to make your very own Hansel and Gretel-style house. To finish, cover the board in shredded coconut to make a snowy scene.

129

afternoon
tea & picnics

Mini Cinnamon & Apple Cakes

MAKES 24 CAKES

½ cup **unsalted butter**, melted and cooled, plus extra for greasing
1 cup **all-purpose flour**
2½ tbsp **cornstarch**
1½ tsp **baking powder**
2 tsp **ground cinnamon**
1 tsp freshly grated **nutmeg**
¼ tsp **salt**
2 large **eggs**
1 cup **light brown sugar**
⅓ cup **whole milk**
2 tsp **vanilla extract**

For the topping
6 large **apples**, preferably Braeburn
juice of 1 **lemon**
7 tbsp **unsalted butter**

For the filling
¾ cup **heavy cream**
½ cup **light brown sugar**

Sometimes you're in the mood to eat a little cake but want something a bit fresher and less sweet than a cupcake. These small spicy cakes fit the bill perfectly. They are filled with a little whipped cream and then topped with some delicious caramelized apples—perfect for a lovely afternoon get-together with friends.

1. Preheat the oven to 350°F and lightly grease two standard 12-cup muffin pans. In a medium bowl whisk the flour, cornstarch, baking powder, cinnamon, nutmeg, and salt together to combine, then set aside.

2. Put the eggs and sugar in a large bowl and whisk together until pale and thickened. Pour in the melted butter and whisk to combine. Add the flour mixture in three additions, alternating with the milk and vanilla, starting and finishing with the flour.

3. Divide the batter among the muffin cups and bake for 12–14 minutes or until a toothpick inserted into the center of a cake comes out clean. Allow the cakes to cool in the pan for 10 minutes before transferring to a wire rack to cool completely.

4. To make the topping, peel, core, and dice the apples, then toss them in the lemon juice to keep them from browning. Put the butter in a medium pan and melt over medium heat, then add the sugar and let dissolve and bubble. Add the apples and cook for a few minutes until slightly softened. Remove from the heat and set aside while you make the filling.

5. Put the cream in a medium bowl and whisk until it holds soft peaks. Make a small hole in the top of each cake using an apple corer or a sharp knife and fill with cream. Top each cake with a small pile of the caramelized apples.

133

Battenburg Cake

MAKES 2 CAKES SERVING 10 EACH

4 large **eggs**
½ tsp **vanilla extract**
¾ tsp **almond extract**.
1⅓ cups **superfine sugar**
¾ cup + 1 tbsp **unsalted butter**, softened
1⅔ cups **all-purpose flour**
1 tsp **baking powder**
red and **yellow food coloring**
confectioners' sugar, to dust
1lb 2oz **marzipan**
½ cup **raspberry jam**, to fill

This recipe comes from a pastry chef friend of mine named Tim Fisher, and to my mind it tastes exactly like the original cake I remember eating as a child. The version here is the classic: an almond-flavored cake with raspberry jam filling. One of the reasons I wanted to include this recipe is that it is a great example of the "high ratio" method, where instead of creaming the butter and sugar you cream the butter with the flour. The result is a cake with a very fine crumb, but one that also stays moist for longer than usual.

1. Preheat the oven to 350°F and lightly grease a 9 × 13in high-sided baking sheet or brownie pan. Take a piece of parchment paper a little longer than the pan and make a horizontal fold across the middle the same height as the pan. Use this to line the brownie pan creating a divide in the center of the pan to keep the two mixtures from running into each other.

2. Put the eggs, vanilla extract, and almond extract in a large bowl with ⅓ cup of the sugar. Using an electric mixer on high speed, beat the eggs until pale and thick. Gradually beat in the remaining sugar, and continue to beat until the eggs are very thick; when the beaters are lifted from the bowl the mixture should form a very thick, slowly dissolving ribbon. Set aside while you prepare the second mixture.

3. Put the butter in a large bowl and sift in the flour and baking powder. Using an electric mixer, cream until light and smooth (it should look a little like cake batter). If your butter isn't soft enough, it will at first look like crumble mixture, but continue beating and eventually the butter and flour will incorporate fully and you will have a smooth batter. Add a quarter of the egg mixture and mix to combine. Repeat with the remaining egg mixture in three additions.

4. Divide the mixture equally between two bowls; this is best done by weight. Add a very small amount of red coloring to one bowl and yellow to the other. Pour the yellow batter into one half of the prepared pan and level it out evenly. Repeat with the pink batter in the second half. Bake for 18–22 minutes or until risen and a toothpick inserted into the center of the cake comes out clean. Allow the cakes to cool in the pan for 15 minutes before turning onto a wire rack to cool completely.

5. Trim the edges off the cakes and cut each cake lengthwise into four equal-sized pieces about 1½in wide. To assemble the cakes, divide the marzipan into two pieces. Dust the work surface with confectioners' sugar and roll out each piece into a 6½ × 11in rectangle or large enough to wrap around a completed cake.

6. Brush the marzipan with a thin layer of raspberry jam and place one yellow and one pink piece of cake onto a piece of parchment paper, sticking the touching sides together with more jam.

7. Lift the cake onto the marzipan and wrap with the marzipan, trimming off any excess. Trim both ends of the cake, to give the Battenberg a neat appearance. Repeat to make a second cake.

TIP

The cake, without the jam or marzipan, freezes very well, so you could make one for eating now and freeze one for another time. Freeze for up to 1 month, wrapped very well with plastic wrap. Thaw in the fridge and then complete as above.

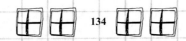

134

Banana Bread

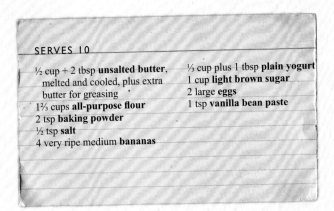

SERVES 10

½ cup + 2 tbsp **unsalted butter**, melted and cooled, plus extra butter for greasing
1⅔ cups **all-purpose flour**
2 tsp **baking powder**
½ tsp **salt**
4 very ripe medium **bananas**

⅓ cup plus 1 tbsp **plain yogurt**
1 cup **light brown sugar**
2 large **eggs**
1 tsp **vanilla bean paste**

The smell of a banana loaf baking is enough to make me feel all warm and cozy—banana bread is for me the ultimate comfort food. If it isn't eaten immediately, one of my favorite ways to enjoy it is sliced and toasted, then spread with a little salted butter. It's so delicious that you might find yourself eating it that way all the time.

1. Preheat the oven to 350°F, and grease and line a 1lb loaf pan with parchment paper. In a medium bowl, mix the flour, baking powder, and salt together. In a large bowl, mash the bananas with the back of a fork until no large lumps remain.

2. Add the yogurt, sugar, eggs, vanilla paste, and melted butter, then mix together until evenly combined. Sift the flour mixture over the yogurt mixture and gently fold together until the dry ingredients are incorporated (don't beat the mixture or the cake will be tough).

3. Pour the mixture into the prepared pan and bake for 1 hour or until risen and golden brown. Allow to cool in the pan for 10 minutes before turning onto a wire rack to cool completely.

TIP

Use very, very ripe bananas—the blacker the better. This way you get that real banana flavor.

Classic Cream Tea

MAKES 10-12

	For the quick raspberry jam
2½ cups **all-purpose flour**, plus extra for dusting	3 cups **raspberries**
1¾ tbsp **baking powder**	2 cups **superfine sugar**
½ tsp **salt**	
3 tbsp **unsalted butter**, diced	
½ cup **superfine sugar**	
⅓ cup plus 1 tbsp **whole milk**	
3 large **eggs**	
½ cup **golden raisins**	
clotted cream (available at specialty supermarkets), to serve	

I grew up visiting Devon, a county in England, a lot as a child, and I was always a big fan of the classic cream tea. Throughout the year my mother would often make scones and they were one of the first things I learned to bake. It was also rare that she bought raspberry jam. We always had raspberries in the freezer, and whenever we needed some jam either for scones or a trifle, she would whip up a batch of her quick raspberry jam. Really, there is little that beats a fresh scone with homemade jam and lashings of clotted cream.

1. To make the raspberry jam, put the raspberries in a large pan and cook for a few minutes over medium-low heat until the fruit begins to release its juice. Stir in the sugar, then cook for a few minutes until the sugar has dissolved. Increase the heat and boil for 10 minutes. Pour the jam into two sterilized jars and seal. Cool and store in the fridge until needed.

2. Line a baking sheet with parchment paper. In a medium bowl whisk the flour, baking powder, and salt together to combine. Add the diced butter and rub into the flour until it resembles fine bread crumbs. Mix in the sugar, then add the milk, 2 of the eggs, and the golden raisins. Using a wooden spoon, mix the ingredients until they just come together and form a soft wet dough.

3. Transfer the dough to a well floured work surface and gently knead by folding the dough in half and then turning it 45 degrees and repeating until the dough is smooth. Be careful not to over-knead the dough—it only needs a very brief, light touch; you're not kneading bread.

4. Lightly flour the surface of the dough and roll out to about 1in thick. Using a 3in plain round cutter, cut out as many scones as you can. Don't twist the cutter when forming the scones but use a firm downward press; this will help the scones rise properly. Make more scones with the trimmings. Put the scones on the baking sheet and allow to rest for 1 hour before baking.

5. Preheat the oven to 400°F. Make an egg wash by mixing the remaining egg and 1 tablespoon water. Brush lightly over the tops of the scones. Try not to get any on the sides, as this will prevent the scones from rising. Bake for 12 minutes or until golden brown on top. Transfer to a wire rack. Serve slightly warm with jam and clotted cream.

MY BROTHER NEIL

Fruit Tarts

MAKES 8

2 cups **all-purpose flour**,
  plus extra for dusting
¼ cup **almond flour**
½ cup **confectioners' sugar**
½ tsp **salt**
seeds from ½ **vanilla bean** or
  1 tsp **vanilla bean paste**
¾ cup **unsalted butter**, chilled
  and diced, plus extra for greasing
1 large **egg yolk**

For the pastry cream filling

1¼ cups **whole milk**
4 large **egg yolks**
2 tbsp **superfine sugar**
1 tbsp **all-purpose flour**
1 tsp **vanilla bean paste**

For the fruit topping

⅔ cup **apricot** or **seedless**
  raspberry jam, sieved
1¼lb **fresh fruit** (such as
  blueberries, raspberries,
  strawberries, cherries)

These little tarts are perfect for a summer afternoon when soft fruits and berries are plentiful and at their best. You can top the tarts them with whatever fruit you'd like, but my favorites are blueberries, strawberries, and raspberries.

1. Put the all-purpose and almond flours, confectioners' sugar, and salt together in the bowl of a food processor and pulse to combine. Add the seeds from the vanilla bean or vanilla bean paste and the butter, and pulse until the mixture resembles coarse bread crumbs. (Alternatively, rub the butter into the flour and vanilla mixture by hand or using a pastry cutter, to resemble coarse bread crumbs.) Mix the egg yolk with 1 tablespoon iced water, then add this to the mixture. Pulse (or stir) until the mixture just comes together, adding a little more water, little by little, if necessary.

2. Transfer to a lightly floured work surface and knead lightly until uniform. Divide the dough in half and wrap in plastic wrap. Chill for at least 30 minutes until ready to use.

3. To make the filling, pour the milk into a medium pan over medium-high heat and bring to a boil. Meanwhile, in a medium bowl, whisk the egg yolks, sugar, and flour until pale and smooth. Once the milk has come to temperature, slowly pour half over the egg mixture, whisking constantly. Pour the egg mixture back into the pan and put back on the heat. Cook over medium heat, whisking constantly, until thickened. Pour the pastry cream into a bowl and stir in the vanilla bean paste. Press a piece of plastic wrap onto the surface to prevent a skin from forming. Cool and chill.

4. Remove the dough from the fridge and let rest for 10 minutes before rolling out. Lightly grease eight 4in tart pans with a little butter and set aside. Roll out the dough on a lightly floured work surface until about ⅛in thick and cut out eight rounds about 5in in diameter. Line the prepared pans with the rounds of dough, trimming away any excess. Line each tart pan with a piece of parchment paper and fill with baking beans or rice. Chill the dough for 10–15 minutes before baking. Preheat the oven to 350°F.

5. Bake the crusts for 15 minutes, then carefully remove the parchment paper and beans and return to the oven for another 10–15 minutes or until the crust is golden. Allow the tarts to cool before removing them from the pans.

6. Warm the jam in a pan over medium heat until dissolved. Fill each tart with a layer of pastry cream. Top each with a little pile of fruit, and brush with a layer of jam. Serve within a few hours of assembling.

Chocolate & Ginger Tarts

MAKES 12

2 cups **all-purpose flour**,
 plus extra for dusting
¼ cup **almond flour**
½ cup **confectioners' sugar**
½ tsp **salt**
¾ cup **unsalted butter**,
 cut into small pieces,
 plus extra for greasing
1 large **egg yolk**
seeds from 1 **vanilla bean**

4 pieces **preserved stem
 ginger** in syrup, drained
 and finely chopped

For the chocolate ganache
8oz **dark chocolate**
 (about 70% cocoa solids),
 finely chopped
¾ cup **heavy cream**
¼ cup **light brown sugar**
3 tbsp **unsalted butter**,
 softened and cut into pieces

These little tarts are pure indulgence and perfect for afternoon tea. They're great if you want to treat someone to something a little bit special. The chocolate and the ginger balance very well and the addition of the light brown sugar tempers the bitterness sometimes associated with dark chocolate.

1. Mix the all-purpose and almond flours, confectioners' sugar, and salt together in a large bowl, then, using your fingertips, rub in the butter until it resembles coarse uneven bread crumbs. Mix the egg yolk and 1 tablespoon ice-cold water together, and add to the bowl with the vanilla seeds, mixing until the dough just comes together. If necessary, gradually add a little more water until you get the correct consistency. Transfer the dough to a lightly floured work surface and knead lightly until just uniform. Flatten into a disc and wrap in plastic wrap. Chill for 30 minutes–1 hour until ready to use.

2. Preheat the oven to 350°F and lightly grease a 12-cup muffin pan. Remove the chilled dough from the fridge and let rest at room temperature for 10 minutes. Lightly flour the work surface and roll out the dough to ⅛in thick. Cut out 12 discs of dough about 4in in diameter, and use to line the prepared muffin cups. Line each tart base with a piece of parchment paper and fill each with a layer of baking beans or rice. Bake for 12–15 minutes, then remove the baking beans and parchment paper, and bake for another 5–10 minutes or until the tarts are golden. Remove from the oven and allow to cool before filling.

3. To make the ganache, put the chocolate in a medium heatproof bowl and set aside. Put the cream and sugar in a small pan over medium heat, bring just to a boil, then remove from the heat and pour in the chocolate. Let stand for a couple of minutes before gently stirring together to form a silky smooth ganache. Add the butter and stir to combine.

4. To assemble the tarts, sprinkle the ginger over the bottom of each tart and top with the chocolate ganache. Let set for 1 hour before serving.

TIP

My favorite way to serve these tarts is to decorate them with a small piece of edible gold leaf and a little whipped cream.

140

Caramelized Banana &
Passion Fruit Tarts

MAKES 12

1lb 2oz **all-butter puff pastry**, thawed if frozen
superfine sugar, to sprinkle

For the passion fruit curd
¾ cup **superfine sugar**
5 large **egg yolks**
⅓ cup sieved **passion fruit purée** (about 5 passion fruit)
7 tbsp **unsalted butter**

For the caramelized bananas
3 medium **bananas**
2 tbsp **unsalted butter**
2½ tbsp **light brown sugar**

I had the idea for these little tarts years ago and they have gone through a few different variations, but this is both the simplest and most satisfying one yet. Banana and passion fruit is a wonderful combination and, trust me, these tarts are seriously addictive.

1. To make the passion fruit curd, put the sugar, egg yolks, and passion fruit purée in a medium pan over medium heat. Whisk the mixture constantly until the curd thickens and is thick enough to coat the back of a spoon. Take the pan off the heat and add the butter, stirring to combine evenly. Pour the curd into a sterilized jar, then cover, cool, and chill until needed.

2. To make the caramelized bananas, first peel and slice the bananas. Put the butter and sugar in a small pan over medium heat and cook until the butter has melted and the sugar has dissolved, and you have a smooth caramel. Cut the banana slices in half and add these to the caramel. Stir to coat evenly, then cook for 2 minutes more. Pour the caramelized banana into a bowl and set aside. Preheat the oven to 400°F and lightly grease a standard 12-cup muffin pan.

3. Roll out the puff pastry into a rectangle ¹/₁₆in thick, and cut out 12 rounds 4in in diameter. Use the pastry rounds to line the prepared muffin pan, then put the pan in the fridge for 15 minutes to let the pastry rest.

4. Prick the bottom of each tart with a fork, then line each with a piece of parchment paper and fill with baking beans or rice. Bake for 15 minutes, then remove the parchment paper and baking beans and put back in the oven to bake for another 5–8 minutes or until golden.

5. Put the muffin pan on a wire rack and allow the tarts to cool. Remove the cooled shells from the pan and fill each with a layer of the caramelized banana and top with a layer of passion fruit curd. Sprinkle with superfine sugar and, using a blowtorch, caramelize the sugar, leaving you with a crème brûlée-like top. (Alternatively, put the tarts under a preheated broiler until the sugar caramelizes; watch carefully as they burn very fast.) These are best served within a couple of hours of assembling.

Cinnamon Rolls

MAKES 16

1 cup **whole milk**
3 tbsp **unsalted butter**,
   plus extra for brushing
3 cups **bread flour**,
   plus extra for dusting
2 tbsp **superfine sugar**
1 tsp **salt**
¼oz **instant yeast**
1 large **egg**

For the filling

¾ cup **light brown sugar**
3 tbsp **ground cinnamon**
4 tbsp **unsalted butter**,
   softened
⅔ cup **currants** (optional)

For the topping

⅔ cup **full-fat cream cheese**
2 cups **confectioners' sugar**
4 tbsp **milk**

The smell of freshly baked cinnamon rolls is the thing that dreams are made of—buttery sweet, spicy dreams! Although they take a little time to make, the preparation time is small and the effort is so worth it. When I make these, I always make sure I get one for myself from the center of the batch. These are softer and, to me, just a little bit more scrumptious.

1. Put the milk and butter in a small pan over low heat. Cook until the butter has melted. Let the mixture stand until it is just lukewarm. In a large bowl, mix together the flour, sugar, salt, and yeast. Add the milk mixture and the egg, and mix to form a soft dough.

2. Lightly flour the work surface and transfer the dough to it. Knead for the dough for 10 minutes or until smooth and elastic. Transfer the dough in a lightly oiled bowl and cover with plastic wrap. Put the bowl in a warm place and let it rise for 1 hour or until doubled in size. Transfer the dough to a lightly floured work surface and roll the dough into a large rectangle, about 15 × 20in. Lightly grease a 9 × 13in high-sided baking sheet or brownie pan.

3. To make the filling, mix the light brown sugar and the cinnamon together. Brush the dough with the softened butter and sprinkle the sugar mixture evenly over it. Sprinkle the currants over the dough and then roll it into a tight log starting from the long edge. Trim off the ends of the rolled dough, then slice the dough into 16 equal pieces. Put the rolls in the greased pan and cover with plastic wrap. Let rise until the rolls have doubled in size, about 45 minutes. Preheat the oven to 350°F.

4. Mix all the topping ingredients together in a medium bowl until smooth. Brush the buns with a little melted butter and bake them for 30 minutes or until golden. To prevent burning you may need to cover the rolls with foil for the last 5–10 minutes. Allow to cool slightly, then pour the topping onto the rolls and spread it to coat evenly. These are best served warm, so dive in and enjoy!

TIP

If you want to make these rolls ready for breakfast, you can cover them with plastic wrap or a damp kitchen towel and chill them overnight, once the dough has been rolled and sliced and put into the pan ready for the final proofing. When ready to bake in the morning, take the rolls out of the fridge about 30 minutes before baking, to bring them to room temperature.

144

Risquits

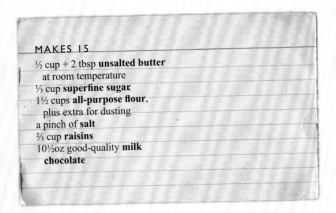

MAKES 15

½ cup + 2 tbsp **unsalted butter**
   at room temperature
⅓ cup **superfine sugar**
1½ cups **all-purpose flour**,
   plus extra for dusting
a pinch of **salt**
⅔ cup **raisins**
10½oz good-quality **milk
   chocolate**

These are total nostalgia for me. They are my version of a chocolate biscuit, or cookie, I sometimes had in my lunchbox when I was in grade school. There was a very well-known TV advertisement for the treat, and I can still remember the theme song today. My version uses a buttery shortbread studded with raisins as the base, hence the name risquits: raisin biscuits.

1. Line a baking sheet with parchment paper. Put the butter and sugar in a medium bowl and beat together until smooth and creamy. Add the flour, salt, and raisins, and mix together until evenly combined. Transfer to a lightly floured work surface and gently knead together until uniform.

2. Roll out the dough to about ½in thick. Cut out fifteen 3½ × 1½in rectangles and put on the prepared baking sheet. Chill for 30 minutes or until the cookies are firm. Preheat the oven to 350°F.

3. Bake for 20–25 minutes or until the edges are golden. Let cool on the baking sheet for 10 minutes before transferring to a wire rack to cool completely.

4. To coat the cookies, have a baking sheet lined with parchment paper ready to use. Melt the chocolate in a heatproof bowl set over a pan of gently simmering water, making sure the bottom of the bowl doesn't touch the water. Remove from the heat and dip the cookies in the chocolate, coating them completely. Use a fork to lift them out and put the coated cookies on the parchment-lined baking sheet to set.

Chocolate-Dipped Flapjacks

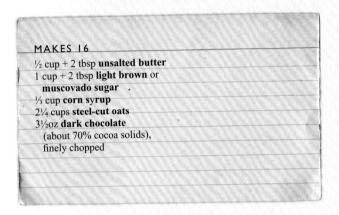

MAKES 16

½ cup + 2 tbsp **unsalted butter**
1 cup + 2 tbsp **light brown** or
  muscovado sugar
⅓ cup **corn syrup**
2¼ cups **steel-cut oats**
3½oz **dark chocolate**
  (about 70% cocoa solids),
  finely chopped

When I was in grade school I remember being picked up after school by my mom, and sometimes as a treat we would go to the bakery in the village, where I would get flapjacks—a delcious chewy cookie made from oats and covered in chocolate. I was one happy seven-year-old!

1. Preheat the oven to 350°F, and line a 9 × 13in baking pan with foil or parchment paper. Put the butter, sugar, and corn syrup in a large pan over medium heat and cook until the butter and sugar have melted and the mixture is smooth.

2. Remove from the heat and pour in the oats. Stir until the oats are coated evenly in the sugar mixture. Pour the flapjack mixture into the prepared pan and press firmly into an even layer. Bake for 20–25 minutes or until the edges are starting to turn golden.

3. Allow to cool completely in the pan before lifting the parchment paper and the flapjack out and cutting into squares. Line a baking sheet with parchment paper. Melt the chocolate in a heatproof bowl set over a pan of gently simmering water, making sure the bottom of the bowl doesn't touch the water. Dip each flapjack into the chocolate, coating half of each piece in chocolate. Set on the parchment paper and chill until the chocolate sets.

147

Lamingtons

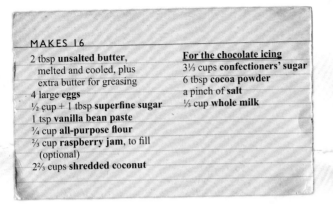

MAKES 16

2 tbsp **unsalted butter**, melted and cooled, plus extra butter for greasing
4 large **eggs**
½ cup + 1 tbsp **superfine sugar**
1 tsp **vanilla bean paste**
¾ cup **all-purpose flour**
⅔ cup **raspberry jam**, to fill (optional)
2⅔ cups **shredded coconut**

For the chocolate icing
3⅓ cups **confectioners' sugar**
6 tbsp **cocoa powder**
a pinch of **salt**
⅓ cup **whole milk**

Australia: home to the kangaroo, the didgeridoo, and the delicious Lamington. It's a simple combination of chocolate, coconut, and sponge cake—just a few ingredients, but we all know that simple is sometimes better. These cakes are great for kids to get involved in making—they can get messy dipping the cakes into the chocolate and rolling them in the coconut.

1. Preheat the oven to 350°F, then grease and line an 8in square cake pan with parchment paper, greasing the parchment too. Put the eggs, sugar, and vanilla paste in a heatproof bowl set over a pan of gently simmering water, making sure the bottom of the bowl doesn't touch the water. Whisk constantly until the sugar has dissolved and the mixture is just warm to the touch.

2. Remove the bowl from the pan and, using an electric mixer, beat for 5 minutes on high speed then reduce to medium and beat for another 3 minutes. By this stage the mixture should have tripled in volume, and when the beaters are lifted from the bowl they should form a slowly dissolving ribbon.

3. Sift in the flour and gently fold together, making sure all the flour is combined but trying to keep as much volume as possible. Take a large spoonful of the batter and add it to the melted butter, then mix together (this will lighten the butter and help to incorporate it into the batter). Gently fold this into the batter.

4. Pour the batter into the prepared pan and gently level out. Bake for 25 minutes or until risen and golden and a skewer inserted into the center of the cake comes out clean. Allow the cake to cool in the pan for 10 minutes before turning onto a wire rack to cool completely.

5. To make the icing, put the confectioners' sugar, cocoa powder, and salt in a medium bowl and mix together. Add the milk and mix until you have a smooth, thin chocolate sauce. Using a serrated knife, slice the cake into 2in squares.

6. For jam-filled Lamingtons, slice the cakes in half through the center and sandwich together with a little raspberry jam. Put the coconut on a large, shallow plate. Dip the cake in the chocolate icing to coat it completely. This might be messy work, but it's fun! Once fully coated, roll in the coconut and set on parchment paper to set.

Dulce de Leche Madeleines

MAKES 12

2 large **eggs**
½ cup **superfine sugar**
⅔ cup **all-purpose flour**,
  plus extra for dusting
½ tsp **baking powder**
7 tbsp **unsalted butter**,
  melted and cooled, plus
  extra butter for greasing

**For the dulce de leche
filling**
1 x 14oz can **dulce de leche**
¼ tsp **sea salt**

Madeleines should be delicious, but store-bought ones can often be disappointing, heavy, and tasteless. But why buy them when they are super-easy to make? To amp up the flavor even more I have filled them with dulce de leche, a milk-based caramel often used in banoffee pie. Once you have eaten them this way you'll probably never want them plain again!

1. Put the eggs and sugar in a large bowl set over a pan of gently simmering water and whisk constantly until the sugar dissolves and the egg mixture is warm. Remove the bowl from the pan and, using an electric mixer, beat on high speed for 5 minutes, reduce the speed to medium, and beat for another 3 minutes.

2. Sift the flour and baking powder over the egg mixture and gently fold together until no streaks of flour remain. Take a large spoonful of the batter and add it to the melted butter, then mix together (this will lighten the butter and help to incorporate it into the batter). Gently fold this into the batter. Cover the bowl with plastic wrap and chill for at least 1 hour or up to two days before using.

3. Preheat the oven to 350°F and grease a standard 12-cup Madeleine pan, making sure to grease all the ridges. (If you don't have a Madeleine pan you could use a 12-cup muffin pan, although of course the shape will differ.) Dust the pan with flour and tap out any excess. Spoon about 1 tablespoon batter into each mold, but don't spread it out; this will happen naturally in the oven. Bake for 12–14 minutes until golden around the edges. Let cool in the pan for 5 minutes before turning onto a wire rack to cool completely.

4. To make the filling, put the dulce de leche and salt in a small pan over medium heat. Stir regularly until the caramel thins out and the salt has dissolved. (This recipe makes more filling then needed, but the extra can be used to pour over ice cream.)

5. Put the filling in a piping bag fitted with a small plain piping tip and press the tip into the end of the Madeleines, squeezing about 1 teaspoon of the caramel into each.

TIP

Dulce de leche is available in most supermarkets, but is sometimes sold as "caramel" and stocked with the condensed and evaporated milks.

Raspberry Ripple Choux Buns

SERVES 8

	For the filling
½ cup plus 1 tbsp **all-purpose flour**	1¼ cups **heavy cream**
4 tbsp **unsalted butter,** cut into small pieces	1 tsp **vanilla bean paste**
¼ tsp **superfine sugar**	1 tbsp **confectioners' sugar,** or to taste, plus extra to taste and for dusting
¼ tsp **salt**	3¼ cups **raspberries**
2–3 large **eggs**	

Raspberry and cream is a wonderful pairing: the tartness of the berries along with the creaminess of the heavy cream. Fill a choux bun with the two and you have a lovely little treat that is also a bit lighter if you're in the mood for something slightly less calorific than a big slice of cake.

1. Preheat the oven to 400°F, and line two baking sheets with parchment paper. Sift a little of the flour onto a sheet of waxed paper. Put the butter, sugar, salt, and ½ cup water in a medium pan over medium-high heat and bring to a rolling boil. Take off the heat and add in the flour. Using a wooden spoon, beat to combine. Put back on the heat and beat the dough for a few minutes or until the dough comes away from the sides of the pan.

2. Transfer the dough to a medium bowl and beat vigorously until no longer steaming. Beat in the eggs, one at a time—you may not need them all; check the consistency of the dough after each addition. It should be smooth and shiny and will fall from the wooden spoon forming a V-shaped ribbon. If it looks almost right after 2 eggs, just add a little of the third and test again. Put the dough in a piping bag fitted with a plain piping tube and pipe into rounds on the prepared baking sheet about 1in in diameter. Using a finger dipped in water, gently tap any peaks down.

3. Bake for 20–25 minutes or until risen and golden brown. Remove the baking sheet from the oven and, using a sharp knife, make a hole in the bottom of each choux bun. Turn the heat off and put the choux buns back into the oven, bottom up, for 10 minutes; this will help keep the buns crisp.

4. To make the filling, put the cream, vanilla paste, and confectioners' sugar in a large bowl and whisk until the cream holds medium-stiff peaks. In a small bowl, mash half the raspberries using the back of a fork and add a little confectioners' sugar, just to sweeten the mixture a little. Fold this mixture into the cream with the remaining raspberries. Slice the choux buns in half and fill with the cream mixture. Dust with a little confectioners' sugar to serve.

154

Pistachio French Crullers

MAKES 12

½ cup plus 1 tbsp **all-purpose flour**
4 tbsp **unsalted butter**, diced
½ tsp **superfine sugar**
¼ tsp **salt**
2–3 large **eggs**
vegetable oil, for deep-frying

For the glaze and topping
¾ cup **confectioners' sugar**
1 tbsp **honey**
1–2 tbsp **milk**
1 cup **pistachios**, shelled and finely chopped

French crullers are a type of doughnut made with choux pastry instead of the usual yeast-based dough or cake batter. In my opinion, these are probably the easiest doughnuts to make. Using choux pastry makes them very light and rather addictive. I have topped the doughnuts with pistachios, but if you want a more classic cruller, just use the glaze.

1. Line two baking sheets with parchment paper and set aside. Sift the flour onto a sheet of waxed paper. Put the butter, sugar, salt, and 1½ cups water in a medium pan over medium-high heat and bring to a rolling boil. Take off the heat and pour in the flour. Using a wooden spoon, beat to just combine. Put back over medium heat and beat the dough for a few minutes or until it comes away from the sides of the pan and leaves a film of dough on the bottom of the pan.

2. Transfer the dough to a medium bowl and beat vigorously until no longer steaming. Beat in the eggs, one at a time—you may not need them all; check the consistency of the dough after each addition. It should be smooth and shiny and will fall from the wooden spoon forming a V-shaped ribbon, but it should be fairly thick rather than runny. If it looks almost right after 2 eggs, just add a little of the third and test again.

3. Put the dough in a piping bag fitted with a large star piping tip and pipe 12 rings of dough onto the prepared baking sheets. Freeze the sheets for 1 hour or until the rings of dough can be peeled off the parchment paper.

4. Make the glaze by mixing the confectioners' sugar, honey, and enough milk to make a thick but pourable glaze. Pour the vegetable oil into a large heavy-bottomed pan up to a depth of 2in and heat to 350–375°F over medium-high heat. When ready to fry the doughnuts, have a baking sheet lined with paper towels ready to drain the excess oil.

5. Put one or two doughnuts into the oil and fry for a few minutes on each side until browned. Use a slotted spoon to remove the doughnuts from the oil and put them on the paper towels. Fry the remaining doughnuts. While they are still warm, dip them in the glaze and then into the pistachios.

TIP

These are best served as fresh as possible and definitely on the day of making.

156

Chocolate Sandwich Cookies

MAKES ABOUT 30

1⅔ cups **all-purpose flour**,
  plus extra for dusting
½ cup **cocoa powder** .
⅔ cup **confectioners' sugar**
¼ tsp **salt**
¾ cup + 1 tbsp **unsalted butter**,
  chilled
1 large **egg**

For the chocolate
ganache filling
4oz **dark chocolate**
  (about 70% cocoa solids),
  finely chopped
½ cup **heavy cream**
2 tbsp **light brown sugar**
2 tbsp **unsalted butter**
  at room temperature,
  cut into small pieces

Most of the cookies in this chapter were taken straight from my childhood, but instead of just recreating the bourbon as I remember, I have made a slightly more grown-up version. The cookie uses something more akin to a pastry dough, and because of this it is lighter and more flaky than the original. I have also filled it with ganache rather than buttercream to make the cookies less like the childhood ones and more fitting to serve with a cup of strong coffee.

1. Line two baking sheets with parchment paper. Put the flour, cocoa powder, confectioners' sugar, and salt into the bowl of a food processor and pulse to combine. Add the butter and pulse until the mixture resembles coarse bread crumbs. (Alternatively, rub the butter into the flour mixture by hand or using a pastry cutter, to resemble coarse bread crumbs.) Add the egg and pulse (or stir) until the mixture just begins to come together.

2. Transfer the mixture to a lightly floured work surface and lightly knead together until uniform. Wrap in plastic wrap and chill for about 1 hour.

3. Remove the dough from the fridge and let stand for a few minutes before rolling. Dust the work surface with a little flour and roll out the dough until it is about ⅛in thick. Using a knife or pizza cutter, cut out rectangles of dough about 2½ × 1¼in and transfer to the prepared baking sheets. Re-roll the scraps to cut out more cookies.

4. Use a fork to prick the cookies a few times; this will prevent them from rising. Put the pans in the fridge for 15–20 minutes or until the dough is firm. Preheat the oven to 350°F.

5. Bake the cookies for 20–25 minutes or until crisp and browning slightly around the edges. Transfer to a wire rack to cool completely before filling.

6. To make the ganache, put the chocolate in a medium heatproof bowl and set aside. Put the cream and sugar in a medium pan over medium heat and bring just to a boil, remove from the heat, and pour in the chocolate. Let stand for a couple of minutes before stirring together to form a silky smooth ganache.

7. Add the butter and stir to combine. Allow the ganache to stand until it has thickened enough to pipe. Fill a piping bag fitted with a small plain piping tube and pipe onto half the cookies. (Alternatively, you can spoon on the ganache.) Sandwich together with a second cookie and allow the ganache to fully set before serving.

CHAPTER FOUR: AFTERNOON TEA & PICNICS

Coconut Macaroon Sandwiches

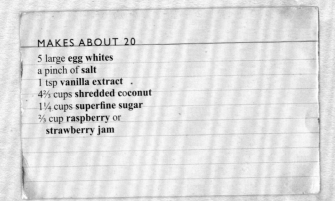

MAKES ABOUT 20

5 large **egg whites**
a pinch of **salt**
1 tsp **vanilla extract** .
4⅔ cups **shredded coconut**
1¼ cups **superfine sugar**
⅔ cup **raspberry** or
  strawberry jam

At my afternoon tea I don't serve real sandwiches. My tea is all about the sweet stuff, so these macaroons are the "savory" course, filled with jam and sliced to look like dainty finger sandwiches.

1. Preheat the oven to 325°F and grease an 8in square cake pan. Line with a strip of parchment paper, leaving a 2in overhang (so that you can remove the macaroon easily) and set aside. Put the egg whites, salt, and vanilla extract into a clean, grease-free bowl and whisk until frothy. Add the coconut and superfine sugar and mix with a wooden spoon until very well combined.

2. Take half the macaroon mixture and press it into the prepared pan, using a spoon to ensure an even, tightly packed layer. Spread the jam evenly over the base layer of coconut and then put spoonfuls of the macaroon mixture across the jam. Use a spoon to level the mixture out, sealing in the jam.

3. Bake for 40 minutes or until the top of the macaroon is a light golden color. Let cool completely in the pan, and then chill for 1 hour. This will firm up the macaroon a little and make it easier to remove and cut.

4. Lift out the macaroon and put onto a cutting board. Using a serrated knife, cut into squares or triangles to look like sandwiches.

Resources

AMAZON

www.amazon.com
Offers a range of bakeware, electrical appliances, and other kitchen gadgets.

FANCY FLOURS

www.fancyflours.com
Online store with a wide selection of bakeware and cake decoration supplies, including cake boards, edible decorations, ribbon, and fondant.

GLOBAL SUGAR ART

www.globalsugarart.com
An online store that ships globally and offers a variety of cake decorating products including rolled fondant cake, gumpaste tools, and molds.

KITCHEN KRAFTS

www.kitchenkrafts.com
Supplier of hard-to-find cooking tools, ingredients, and supplies.

WILTON

www.wilton.com
Offers a variety of Wilton bakeware along with a range of cake and cookie decorating supplies.

STYROFOAM CONES

You can buy small styrofoam cones at craft stores such as: **www.michaels.com** but if you need a larger cone like the one I used for my macaron tower then you can get custom-sized cones from **www.grahamsweet.com,** a UK-based seller.

EDIBLE FLOWERS

www.waitrose.com
www.freshorigins.com
You should get your edible flowers from a supplier who can guarantee that the flowers didn't come into contact with pesticides.

BUNDT/BUNDLETTE PANS

I prefer those made by Nordic Ware and they are available at most department stores and all good cookshops including the ones mentioned above.

175

Thank you

First and foremost my thanks go to Matt—you put up with me for months while I made a mess of our kitchen and constantly fed you cake. Thanks for being a huge support and for calming me down when I got stressed. I love you very much.

Thank you to everyone in my family who dug into the photo albums looking for lots of old pictures of family occasions—it was great to see them and to remember forgotten events.

Thanks to everyone at Kyle Books, especially Kyle and Catharine. I really think this is a beautiful book and it's because of your continued support that I got to write it.

Working on the photography was so much fun and I love the results. Georgia, you did an amazing job, I couldn't be happier—thanks for a fun-filled few weeks. Anna and Emily, thank you for making me laugh and making my food look delicious—working with you both was brilliant. Anita, you took my idea and ran away with it. I am thrilled with the design—thank you so much.

And thank you to everyone who bought my first book and for picking up this one. I love writing the books and I hope you enjoy baking from them.

Happy Baking!

Edd

MY WONDERFUL GRANDPARENTS